QUIZ QUEST 1

QUIZ QUEST 1

KINGFISHER

BOSTON

KINGFISHER

a Houghton Mifflin Company imprint
222 Berkeley Street
Boston, Massachusetts 02116
www.houghtonmifflinbooks.com

First published in 2006
10 9 8 7 6 5 4 3 2 1

1TR/0606/LFG/PICA(PICA)/140MA/C

Senior editor: Jane Chapman
Editor: Conrad Mason
Coordinating editor: Stephanie Pliakas
Senior designer: Steve Woosnam-Savage
Picture research manager: Cee Weston-Baker
Artbank archivist: Wendy Allison
Production manager: Nancy Roberts
DTP coordinator: Catherine Hibbert

ISBN-13: 978-0-7534-6042-9
ISBN-10: 0-7534-6042-4

Printed in China

Contents

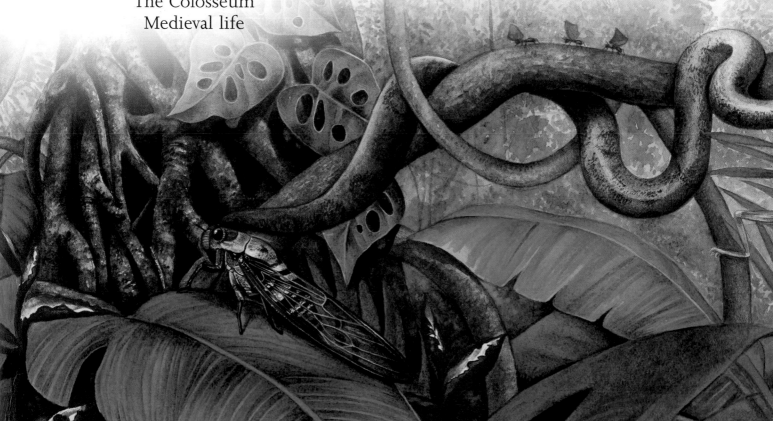

How this book works

It's as easy as one, two, three! Option one: use the question panels to quiz yourself. Option two: turn the page to read all about the topic—the numbered circles show you where to look to figure out the answer for yourself. Option three: look up the answers at the back of the book. These are the three ways that you can use *Quiz Quest*. Or you can just read the book all the way through!

1. The questions
Look at the question panel on the right-hand side of each page. You will find the questions divided into three levels of difficulty. Level 1 questions are easy, Level 2 are harder, and Level 3 are real brainteasers! Stumped? There are two ways to find the answer.

2. Read all about it!
You can turn the page and read all about the quiz topic. Look for the number of each question in the colored circles—the answer will be somewhere inside that box . . .

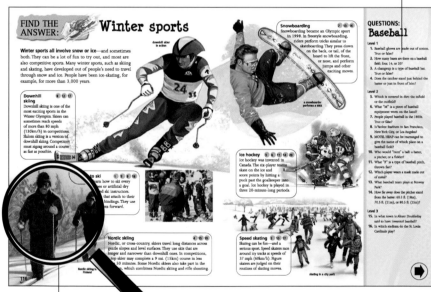

3. The answers
. . . Or, you can look up the answers at the back of the book. Just turn to the right topic and find out whether you got them right.

Picture clues
You can find clues to some of the answers in the pictures. Look at them to try to figure out the answers.

Quick quiz
The answer pages have the questions too, so you can ask a friend to give you a quick quiz—another great way to use *Quiz Quest*!

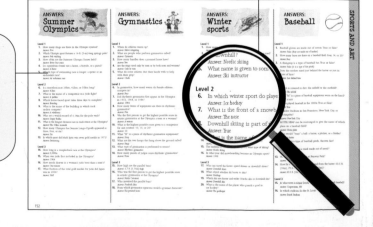

QUIZ ONE
Nature

QUESTIONS:
The rain forest

Level 1

1. Are frogs reptiles or amphibians?
2. Are reptiles cold-blooded or warm-blooded?
3. The world's largest river begins with "A." What is it?
4. How often does it usually rain in the rain forest: daily, weekly, or monthly?

Level 2

5. In which continent does the cinchona tree grow?
6. What type of animal is a boa?
7. Which plant has the largest flower in the world?
8. In which part of the rain forest do most of its animals live?
9. What do pitcher plants feed on?
10. What does the flower of the rafflesia plant smell like?
11. GREEN STEM can be rearranged to give the name of which group of tall trees?
12. Where in the world do poison dart frogs live?
13. Is a bromeliad an animal or a plant?
14. A poison dart frog's skin has enough poison to kill a person. True or false?
15. Where does the atlas moth live?

Level 3

16. Are snakes more closely related to frogs or lizards?
17. How wide is the Amazon river at its mouth: more than 185 mi. (300km), more than 250 mi. (400km), or more than 300 mi. (500km)?
18. What illness is treated with quinine?
19. What part of geckos' bodies gives them a good grip?
20. Where do plants known as epiphytes grow?

FIND THE ANSWER:  The rain forest

The tropical rain forest is the richest of all natural habitats. More animals and plants live there than anywhere else on Earth. The rain forest is well named—in most places it rains every day. The mixture of water and warmth is what makes this habitat so full of life.

emergents

parrots

monkey

Canopy 8 11
The canopy is like the roof of the rain forest, formed by the branches of the tallest trees. Most rain-forest animals live there, eating leaves, flowers, and fruits—or each other. Very tall trees, called emergents, rise above the top of the canopy.

toucan

jaguar

Plants 13 20
Rain-forest trees are themselves covered with other plants. Climbers, such as vines and strangler figs, grip their trunks, while ferns and bromeliads grow in their branches. Plants that grow on other plants in this way are called epiphytes.

Insects 15
Rain-forest insects include the world's largest moth—the atlas moth, which lives in the rain forests of Southeast Asia.

Reptiles 2 6 16 19
Reptiles are cold-blooded animals that thrive in the warmth of tropical rain forests. Snakes, such as boas and pythons, hunt prey in the branches, while geckos scamper up and down the trunks, gripping with their flattened toes, which act a little bit like suction cups.

common lancehead

Amphibians 1 12 14
The dampness of the rain forest suits slimy-skinned amphibians such as the poison dart frog of South America. This type of frog has enough poison in its skin to kill a person.

Swiss cheese plant

red-eyed tree frog

heliconia flower

cicada

poison dart frog

Rivers ③ ⑰

Almost all of the world's largest rivers flow through rain forests. Among them is the largest river of all, the Amazon. This massive waterway drains most of the continent of South America. Close to its mouth in Brazil, the Amazon river is more than 185 mi. (300km) wide.

Plants and animals ⑦ ⑨ ⑩

Rain-forest plants use animals in unusual ways. Pitcher plants lure insects inside their "pitchers" with drops of nectar. They then digest the insects as food. The rafflesia has the world's largest flower—3 ft. (1m) wide. It smells like rotten meat in order to attract flies to pollinate it.

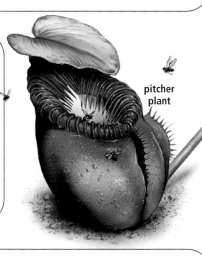

pitcher plant

Water ④

Plants have adapted in different ways to the daily downpours of the rain forests. Many have shiny leaves with downward-pointing tips to channel away water. Some, growing in branches, have trailing roots to gather rain running off the trees.

Plant remedies ⑤ ⑱

Many medicines were first discovered in rain-forest plants. Quinine, for example, is used to treat malaria. It was first taken from the bark of the cinchona tree, which grows in South American rain forests.

QUESTIONS:
Ants

Level 1

1. Which have stronger mandibles (jaws): worker or soldier ants?
2. What "Q" is the large ant that lays all of the eggs in a colony?
3. Are aphids worms or insects?
4. Are wood ants bigger or smaller than most other ants?

Level 2

5. Are there any ants that bring aphids inside their nests?
6. Most ants build nests underground. True or false?
7. What do aphids feed on?
8. What is the name of the sugary substance that aphids produce?
9. Are honeypot ants most common in dry or wet places?
10. Do leaf-cutters live in warm or cold forests?
11. Do wood ants ever bite people?
12. What type of substance can some ants fire at attackers?
13. What do wood ants build their nests from?
14. Do ants ever attack birds?

Level 3

15. Do leaf-cutters eat the leaves that they harvest?
16. How many different types of ants are there in a colony?
17. What does the word "metamorphose" mean?
18. In what type of forest do most wood ants live?
19. Do all of the workers in a honeypot ant colony store food inside their bodies?
20. Name a continent in which both honeypot ants and leaf-cutters live.

FIND THE ANSWER:  Ants

Ants live in huge communities of closely related individuals. Most ants are workers, collecting food and caring for the eggs and larvae (young). Soldier ants are slightly larger than workers and protect the nest from intruders. All ants are hatched from eggs laid by a giant ant called the queen.

Farming   3 5 7 8
Some ants farm smaller insects called aphids. Aphids feed on plant sap and produce a sugary substance called honeydew, which the ants eat. Some ants bring aphids inside their nests to feed them so that the ants can eat the honeydew.

Eggs   2 16 17
All of the eggs in an ants' nest are laid by the queen and are then taken away by worker ants to special chambers. There they are tended until they hatch. The worker ants feed the newly hatched larvae until they are big enough to metamorphose (change shape) into adult ants themselves.

Leaf-cutters   10 15 20
These ants live in warm forests in North and South America. They gather leaves as compost to grow mushrooms (fungi), which they eat.

Tunnels   6
Most ants build their nests underground for protection from the weather and predators. They dig tunnels and chambers in soft soil.

entrance to the nest

aphids

worker ant

queen ant

larvae

10

Attack and defense

 1 12 14 16

Soldier ants are larger than workers and have stronger mandibles, or jaws, so their job is to protect the colony from attacks. Worker ants join in if needed. Some ants also defend themselves by firing acid from the rear sections of their bodies. Ants are fearless and often attack much larger insects for food. They will swarm over birds or mammals if they threaten the ants' nest.

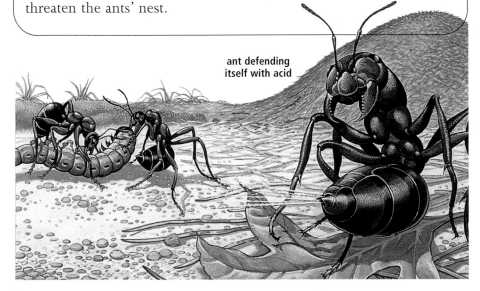

ant defending itself with acid

Honeypot ants 9 19 20

These ants use some of their workers as storage jars. They feed the storage ants with nectar, which is held inside their bodies for future use. Honeypot ants live in dry regions in North and South America, Africa, and Australia.

Wood ants 4 11 13 18

Wood ants live in pine forests and make their nests above the ground. They build them from dried pine needles, which they collect from the forest floor. Their nests can be more than 3 ft. (1m) high. Wood ants are bigger than most ant species (types). Their mandibles are so large that they will even bite people if they are disturbed.

QUESTIONS:
Dinosaurs

Level 1

1. What did *Spinosaurus* have on its back: wings or a sail?
2. What "S" was the largest stegosaur?
3. Which dinosaur had plates on its back: *Kentrosaurus* or *Tyrannosaurus rex*?
4. Which had larger teeth: plant-eating or meat-eating dinosaurs?

Level 2

5. *Tyrannosaurus rex* teeth could be almost 4 in. (10cm) long. True or false?
6. Do fossils take thousands or millions of years to form?
7. Did sauropods have long necks or short necks?
8. Did any dinosaurs have beaks?
9. What did *Styracosaurus* have on its nose?
10. What did male horned dinosaurs probably use their horns for, besides defense?
11. Which are more common: scattered fossil bones or entire fossil skeletons?
12. What type of dinosaur was *Kentrosaurus*?
13. How did a *Spinosaurus* cool down?
14. Where can you see dinosaur bones on display?

Level 3

15. What did *Tyrannosaurus rex* eat?
16. Which was bigger: *Seismosaurus* or *Stegosaurus*?
17. Are fossils made out of bone or of minerals from rocks?
18. *Styracosaurus* ate meat. True or false?
19. Is an *Apatosaurus* more closely related to a *Seismosaurus* or a *Styracosaurus*?
20. How many rows of plates did most stegosaurs have?

FIND THE ANSWER: Dinosaurs

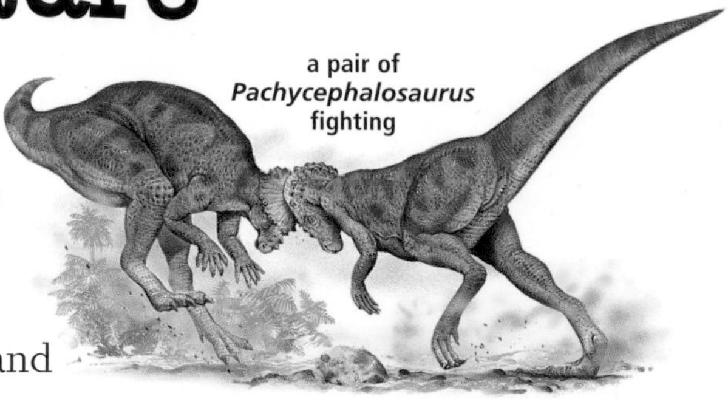

a pair of *Pachycephalosaurus* fighting

Dinosaurs first appeared on Earth 235 million years ago but were all wiped out suddenly 170 million years later, probably by a massive asteroid (rock from space) that hit Earth. Dinosaurs are the ancestors of modern-day reptiles and birds and included the largest land animals ever. Some close relatives of dinosaurs also lived in the sea and flew in the air.

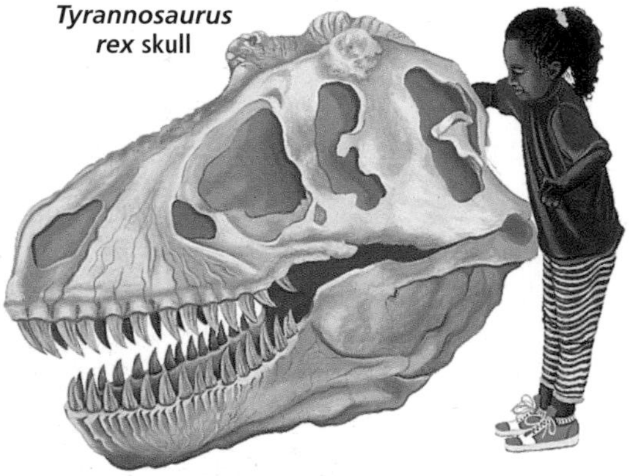

fossilized *Tyrannosaurus rex* skull

Food 4 5 8 15

Some dinosaurs ate meat, and others ate plants. Plant eaters had small, peglike teeth, and some had horny beaks. Meat eaters had large, sharp teeth for slicing flesh. A *Tyrannosaurus rex* tooth could be more than 5 in. (15cm) long!

Apatosaurus

Fossils 6 17

Fossils are formed over millions of years, when a dead dinosaur's bones are buried under mud or sand and are slowly replaced with minerals from the surrounding rocks.

Sails 1 13

The *Spinosaurus* had a large "sail" on its back. In hot weather, it could pump blood into the sail in order to cool itself down.

Defense 9 10 18

Many plant eaters had horns to protect themselves from big meat eaters. This *Styracosaurus* had one on his nose. Male horned dinosaurs may also have used their horns to fight each other, just like male cattle and antelope do today.

Spinosaurus

Oviraptor

Stygimoloc

Styracosaurus

Panoplosaurus

Giant dinosaurs (7) (16) (19)

The biggest dinosaurs of all were plant-eating sauropods like this *Apatosaurus*. Sauropods all had small heads on long necks. The largest, such as the giant *Seismosaurus*, could sometimes weigh more than 100 tons.

Skeletons (11) (14)

Most dinosaur fossils are just a few scattered bones, but sometimes complete skeletons are found. They can then be pieced together on metal frames to be displayed in museums.

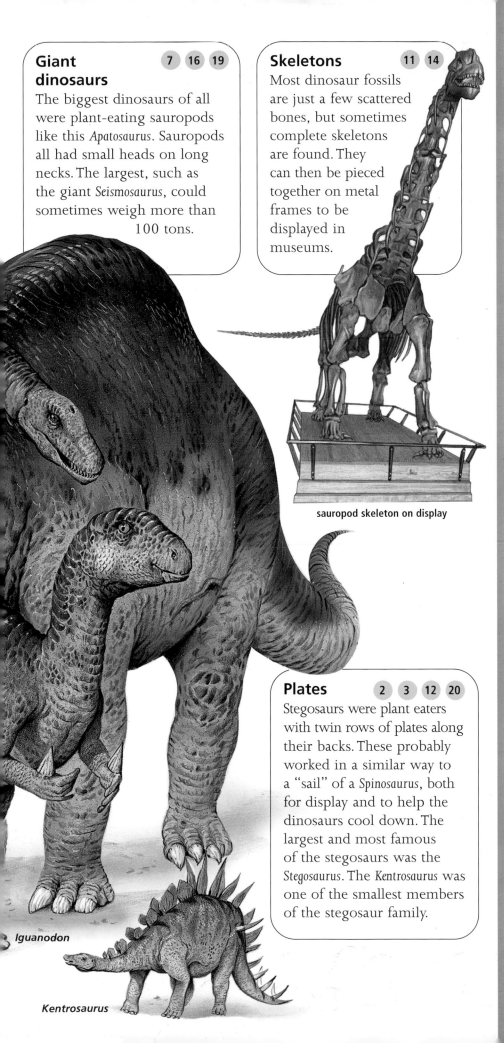

sauropod skeleton on display

Iguanodon

Kentrosaurus

Plates (2) (3) (12) (20)

Stegosaurs were plant eaters with twin rows of plates along their backs. These probably worked in a similar way to a "sail" of a *Spinosaurus*, both for display and to help the dinosaurs cool down. The largest and most famous of the stegosaurs was the *Stegosaurus*. The *Kentrosaurus* was one of the smallest members of the stegosaur family.

QUESTIONS:
Snakes

Level 1

1. Are pythons snakes?
2. Do snakes have legs?
3. Can snakes see?

Level 2

4. Are there any snakes that eat eggs?
5. Which snakes have a hood that they raise when threatened?
6. Where is a rattlesnake's rattle: in its mouth or on the end of its tail?
7. Are snakes vertebrates or invertebrates?
8. What are snakes' skeletons made from?
9. Do snakes' eggs have hard or flexible shells?
10. Are there any snakes that give birth to live young?
11. Rattlesnakes live in Africa. True or false?
12. Do cobras have solid or hollow fangs?
13. Do anacondas grow to more than 19 in. (50cm) long, more than 9 ft. (3m) long, or more than 26 ft. (8m) long?
14. Does camouflage make a snake harder or easier to see?

Level 3

15. What does a baby snake have on its snout to help it hatch?
16. Why do snakes flick their tongues in and out?
17. How do snakes move?
18. How do pythons kill their prey?
19. What does the African egg-eating snake use to break eggs?

FIND THE ANSWER: Snakes

Snakes are reptiles like tortoises, turtles, and lizards.
Reptiles are cold-blooded animals, which means that their body temperatures change according to their surroundings. Because they need warmth to be active, most snakes live in hot countries.

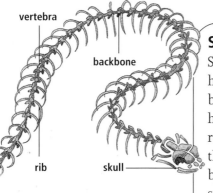
vertebra
backbone
rib
skull

Skeleton 2 7 8 17
Snakes are vertebrates and have skeletons made of bone. Snakes have no legs, however, and move by rippling the muscles on the undersides of their bodies. A snake's body is supported by its many ribs.

Eggs 9 10 15
Most snakes lay eggs, although some give birth to live young. Unlike birds' eggs, snakes' eggs have flexible, leathery shells. Baby snakes have a sharp egg tooth on their snouts for breaking out of their eggs.

Food 4 19
Almost all snakes are predators that catch and eat live animals. A few specialize in eating eggs. The African egg-eating snake dislocates its jaws to swallow birds' eggs that are three times larger than its head. The egg is swallowed whole and is punctured by sharp spines that stick down from the snake's backbone.

coral snake moving by rippling its muscles

cobra

Cobras 5 12
These large snakes kill their prey with venom. They inject this poisonous liquid into their victims through their hollow fangs. Cobras can easily be told apart from other snakes by the hoods that they have behind their heads. When they feel threatened, they raise themselves up and spread their hoods outward, just like this cobra is doing.

Senses ③ ⑯

Snakes are able to see, but their senses of smell and taste are combined. Snakes flick their tongues in and out because they can taste the air. A snake's forked tongue can pick up particles given off by prey, and these are detected by an organ, called the Jacobson's organ, in the roof of the snake's mouth.

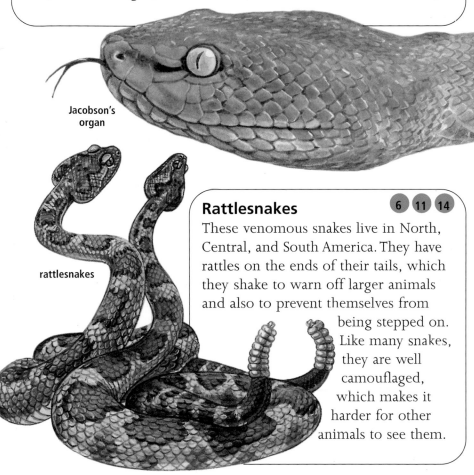

Jacobson's organ

rattlesnakes

Rattlesnakes ⑥ ⑪ ⑭

These venomous snakes live in North, Central, and South America. They have rattles on the ends of their tails, which they shake to warn off larger animals and also to prevent themselves from being stepped on. Like many snakes, they are well camouflaged, which makes it harder for other animals to see them.

Constrictor ① ⑬ ⑱

Some snakes, such as boas and pythons, are called constrictors because they wrap themselves around their prey until it suffocates. Anacondas are constrictors from the Amazon region of South America. They reach more than 26 ft. (8m) long.

garter snake

prey is squeezed to death

QUESTIONS:
Sharks

Level 1

1. Are sharks fish or reptiles?
2. The whale shark is the world's biggest fish. True or false?
3. Do great white sharks eat lions or sea lions?
4. Is a shark's egg case called a mermaid's purse or a sailor's purse?

Level 2

5. Do sharks have the same set of teeth throughout their lives?
6. Do basking sharks live in warmer or cooler water than whale sharks?
7. The biggest great white sharks can grow up to 20 ft. (6m) long. True or false?
8. What is the name given to the tiny sea creatures that are food for whale sharks?
9. Which is bigger: the basking shark or the great white shark?
10. HE MADE HARM can be rearranged to give the name of which type of shark?
11. How heavy can a whale shark be: 11 tons, 21 tons, or 31 tons?
12. Do all sharks lay eggs?
13. The teeth of an individual shark are all the same shape. True or false?
14. Which shark is more likely to attack people: the great white or the hammerhead?
15. Do sharks ever resort to cannibalism (eating each other)?

Level 3

16. What feature of a hammerhead makes it easier to follow a scent trail in the water?
17. The second-largest shark in the world is found off the U.S. What is this?
18. What is the largest shark to actively hunt prey?

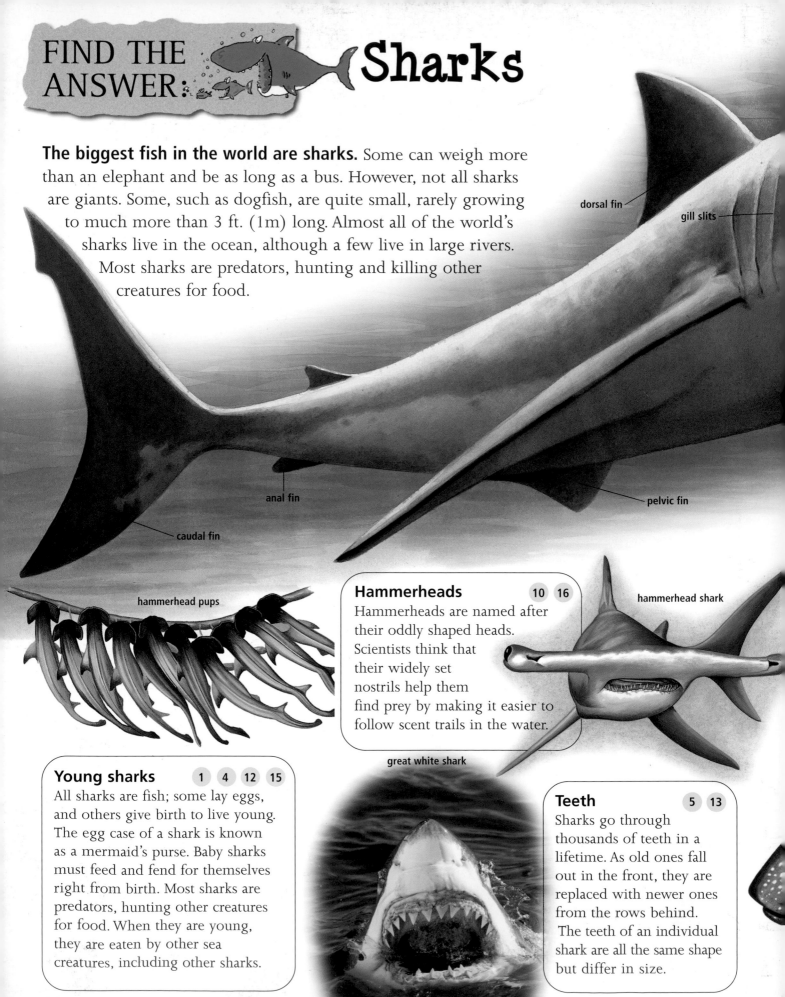

Sharks

The biggest fish in the world are sharks. Some can weigh more than an elephant and be as long as a bus. However, not all sharks are giants. Some, such as dogfish, are quite small, rarely growing to much more than 3 ft. (1m) long. Almost all of the world's sharks live in the ocean, although a few live in large rivers. Most sharks are predators, hunting and killing other creatures for food.

dorsal fin

gill slits

anal fin

pelvic fin

caudal fin

hammerhead pups

Hammerheads   10   16
Hammerheads are named after their oddly shaped heads. Scientists think that their widely set nostrils help them find prey by making it easier to follow scent trails in the water.

hammerhead shark

great white shark

Young sharks   1   4   12   15
All sharks are fish; some lay eggs, and others give birth to live young. The egg case of a shark is known as a mermaid's purse. Baby sharks must feed and fend for themselves right from birth. Most sharks are predators, hunting other creatures for food. When they are young, they are eaten by other sea creatures, including other sharks.

Teeth   5   13
Sharks go through thousands of teeth in a lifetime. As old ones fall out in the front, they are replaced with newer ones from the rows behind. The teeth of an individual shark are all the same shape but differ in size.

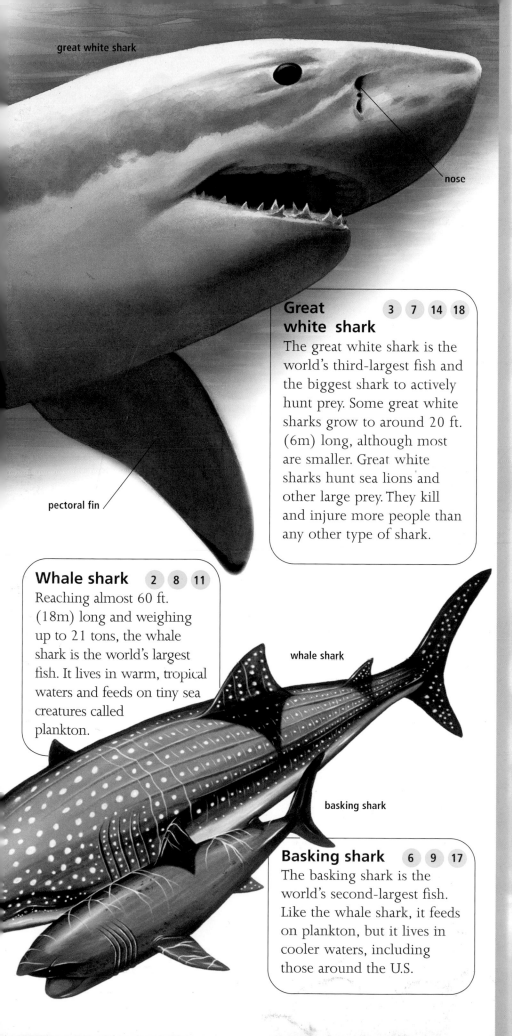

great white shark

nose

pectoral fin

Great white shark 3 7 14 18

The great white shark is the world's third-largest fish and the biggest shark to actively hunt prey. Some great white sharks grow to around 20 ft. (6m) long, although most are smaller. Great white sharks hunt sea lions and other large prey. They kill and injure more people than any other type of shark.

Whale shark 2 8 11

Reaching almost 60 ft. (18m) long and weighing up to 21 tons, the whale shark is the world's largest fish. It lives in warm, tropical waters and feeds on tiny sea creatures called plankton.

whale shark

basking shark

Basking shark 6 9 17

The basking shark is the world's second-largest fish. Like the whale shark, it feeds on plankton, but it lives in cooler waters, including those around the U.S.

QUESTIONS:
Sea creatures

Level 1

1. How many tentacles does an octopus have?
2. Most of a jellyfish's body is made up of air. True or false?
3. What does scuba equipment help people to do?
4. Are sea horses fish or mollusks?

Level 2

5. What is the world's largest species of ray?
6. Are there more than 100 types of sharks in the world?
7. How many tentacles does a squid have?
8. What do squid eat: jellyfish, plankton, or fish?
9. What do jellyfish use to attack their prey?
10. Are squid invertebrates?
11. Which ocean habitat is home to the most types of fish?
12. How long can divers stay underwater for: ten minutes or more, 15 minutes or more, or 20 minutes or more?
13. What do the tanks in scuba equipment contain?
14. Are sharks more closely related to squid or rays?
15. Do squid spend most of their time in open water or on the seabed?

Level 3

16. What "P" leaves behind the hard, stony cases that we see in coral reefs?
17. To which of these creatures are corals most closely related: jellyfish, giant clams, or sharks?
18. What word is used to describe a tail that can grip things?

Sea creatures

jellyfish

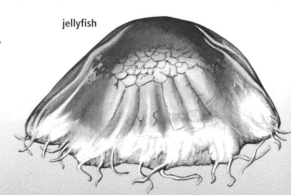

Most of the world's animals live in the sea. The sea itself covers more than two thirds of the planet's surface. Sea creatures vary greatly in shape, size, and type. Most, however, fall into two groups: vertebrates and invertebrates. Vertebrates are animals that have a backbone, like people do. Invertebrates don't have any bones.

Sharks 5 6 14
Altogether, there are more than 360 different species (types) of sharks. Sharks are closely related to rays. The world's largest ray, a manta ray, can be seen in this picture just below the squid.

Jellyfish 2 9 17
Jellyfish are invertebrates with simple body structures, closely related to corals. More than 90 percent of a jellyfish is water. Jellyfish hunt other animals with their stinging tentacles.

Squid 1 7 8 10 15
Squid swim in open water and hunt fish and small sea creatures. They are closely related to octopuses but, unlike them, have ten tentacles instead of eight. Both are cephalopods (a type of invertebrate).

hammerhead shark

great white shark

Corals 16
Corals often crowd together to form reefs. The parts we usually see are hard, stony cases laid down by individual polyps: tiny sea-anemone-like animals.

starfish

giant clam

corals

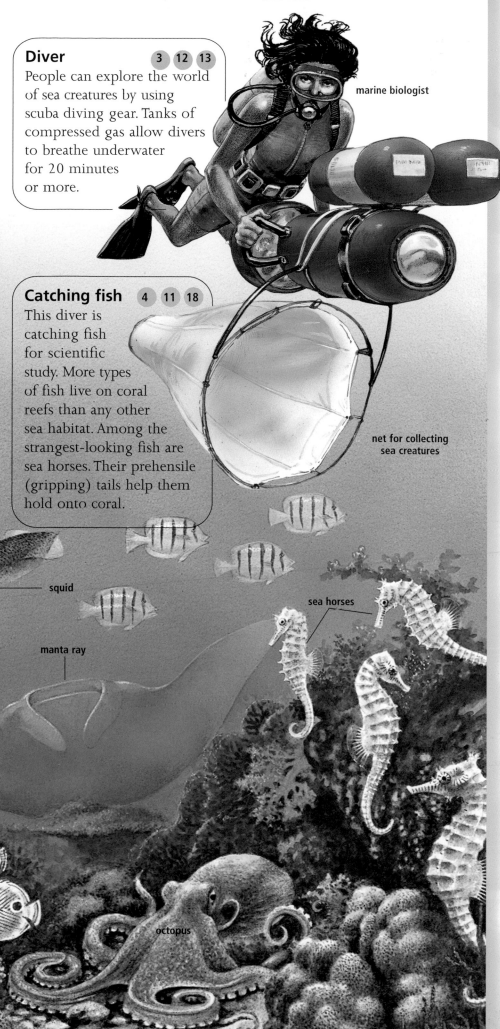

Diver 3 12 13
People can explore the world of sea creatures by using scuba diving gear. Tanks of compressed gas allow divers to breathe underwater for 20 minutes or more.

marine biologist

Catching fish 4 11 18
This diver is catching fish for scientific study. More types of fish live on coral reefs than any other sea habitat. Among the strangest-looking fish are sea horses. Their prehensile (gripping) tails help them hold onto coral.

net for collecting sea creatures

squid

manta ray

sea horses

octopus

QUESTIONS:
Marine mammals

Level 1
1. What is the biggest animal on Earth: the elephant or the blue whale?
2. Do seals eat fish or seaweed?
3. By what name are orcas more commonly known: killer whales or seals?
4. Baby harp seals are born with gray fur. True or false?

Level 2
5. Which use echolocation to find their prey: dolphins or walrus?
6. What "K" are shrimplike creatures that humpback whales eat?
7. Seals give birth in the sea. True or false?
8. Do all walrus have tusks or just males?
9. What "P" is a group of killer whales known as?
10. Why are many large whales rare today?
11. Which marine mammals sometimes kill and eat whales that are larger than they are?
12. Do all whales eat large animals?
13. Which ocean surrounds the North Pole?
14. What "S" do walrus eat?

Level 3
15. Where on a whale would you find its baleen?
16. What "C" is the name of the marine mammal group that contains whales and dolphins?
17. Near which pole do walrus live: the North Pole or the South Pole?
18. What part of a blue whale weighs as much as an elephant?
19. How long was the largest blue whale ever measured?

FIND THE ANSWER:

Marine mammals

Mammals are warm-blooded animals that feed milk to their young. Most live on land, but some, the marine mammals, live in the sea. Marine mammals include whales, dolphins, seals, sea lions, and walrus. All of them breathe air but have adapted to life in the water, having flippers instead of legs, for example.

blue whale's size compared to other animals

Biggest animal   1 18 19

The blue whale is the biggest animal that has ever lived. Its heart is as big as a car, and its tongue weighs as much as an elephant. The biggest ever measured was 110 ft. (33.5m) long.

Killer whales   3 9 11

Killer whales, or orcas, live and hunt in groups called pods. By working together, they can overpower and kill much larger whales. Some orcas hunt small prey like seals and fish.

killer whale pod attacking a humpback whale

Humpbacks   6 12 15

Like most large whales, humpbacks feed on small fish and shrimplike krill. They trap whole schools of fish inside their mouths behind plates of baleen, which hang down from their upper jaws.

humpback whale

whaling ship harpooning a humpback whale

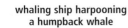

Whaling   10

Most large whales are rare because they were hunted in the past. Whalers killed them for their meat, which is considered a delicacy in some countries. It is now illegal to hunt most large whales, and the huge whaling fleets that once sailed the seas are a thing of the past.

Dolphins   ⑤ ⑯

Like whales, dolphins belong to a mammal group called the cetaceans. Dolphins use echolocation to find food, making loud clicks and then listening for the echoes that bounce back. They often work together to round up prey.

bottle-nosed dolphins

Seals   ② ④ ⑦

Seals eat fish, but they pull themselves out onto ice or land to rest and give birth to their young. Baby harp seals are born with white coats. Their mothers' milk is very thick and creamy.

baby harp seal with its mother

walrus tusks

Walrus   ⑧ ⑬ ⑭ ⑰

The walrus lives in the Arctic Ocean, which surrounds the North Pole. It feeds on shellfish, which it collects from the seabed. All walrus have long tusks, although those of the males are bigger. They use their tusks to compete for mates and also to defend themselves from polar bears. Walrus live together in large groups.

QUESTIONS:
Seabirds

Level 1

1. Do puffins carry food in their mouths, on their feet, or on their wings?
2. Do seagulls ever feed inland?
3. SNIFF UP can be rearranged to give the name of which seabirds?
4. An albatross is a type of seabird. True or false?
5. What "F" is the main food of most seabirds?

Level 2

6. Some seabirds carry food for their chicks inside their stomachs. True or false?
7. Why do cormorants stand with their wings open after hunting in the water?
8. Do puffins use their wings or feet to swim?
9. Do boobies hunt by diving into the water from the air or by diving in from the surface?
10. Is a male frigate bird's throat pouch red, yellow, or blue?
11. Do cormorants use their wings or feet to swim?
12. Does oil float on water, or does it sink?
13. Do frigate birds live in the tropics or near the North Pole?

Level 3

14. What "G" is a seabird that nests near the tops of cliffs?
15. What does the word "regurgitate" mean?
16. How do frigate birds get food?
17. Why do male frigate birds inflate their throat pouches with air?
18. What "T" is a word for the warm air currents that frigate birds use in order to lift them into the air?

Seabirds

Many birds find their food in the ocean. Birds that do this are known as seabirds. Shore birds, such as the oystercatcher, live near the sea and find their food on mudflats and beaches. Although seabirds spend their lives out over the ocean, they lay their eggs on land and return every year to coastal cliffs to breed.

Frigate birds   10 13 16 17

Frigate birds live in the tropics and attack other seabirds in order to steal their food. Males have red throat pouches, which they inflate to attract females.

Colonies   14

Many types of seabirds live and breed in large colonies on cliffs in order to help protect each other from predators. The gannet, shown on the right, nests near the tops of cliffs.

Food   1 5 6 15

Most seabirds eat fish and carry it back to their chicks. Some, such as puffins, stuff their beaks with food. Others swallow it and then regurgitate it (cough it up) when they return.

Hunting   3 8 9

The booby dives from the air into the water to catch its prey. Other seabirds, such as puffins, land on the water and dive in from the surface, paddling with their wings.

gannet

tern

red-billed tropic bird dropping its prey

frigate birds attacking

booby diving

oystercatcher

shearwater

puffin

booby snatching its prey

Cormorant
7 11

Cormorants are large seabirds that hunt by diving from the water's surface and using their webbed feet as paddles. After hunting, they stand with their wings held wide-open in order to dry off their feathers.

cormorant drying its wings

Using air currents
4 18

Some seabirds, such as frigate birds, use thermals (warm air currents) to lift them into the air. Others, such as the albatross, use small updrafts that blow off the crests of waves to lift them upward.

On land and in the sea
2

Some seabirds have become successful on land as well as in the ocean. Many seagulls, for example, have learned to find food in garbage cans and at dumps. They also follow fishing boats for discarded fish.

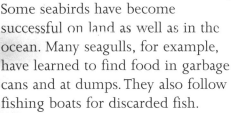

Pollution
12

Seabirds often suffer because of human waste and pollution. Whenever oil tankers sink, hundreds of seabirds die as the oil floats on the water and clogs up their feathers. Only the lucky ones that are found on beaches and are cleaned up can survive.

QUESTIONS:
Birds

Level 1

1. Do birds have teeth?
2. Birds are the only animals in the world that have feathers. True or false?
3. Do birds flap their wings when they are gliding?
4. Can swans fly?

Level 2

5. A NEST FILM can be rearranged to give the name of what parts of a feather?
6. What is the world's largest bird?
7. Birds have elbow joints. True or false?
8. Are birds' bones solid or hollow?
9. GLEAM UP can be rearranged to give what name for the feathers that cover a bird?
10. Does a kestrel eat fruit, seeds, or meat?
11. Which are usually more brightly colored: male birds or female birds?
12. Which "H" means to stay still in midair?
13. Which has a longer beak: a curlew or a robin?
14. How many times can hummingbirds flap their wings every second: seven times, 70 times, or 700 times?

Level 3

15. What is the chamber between a bird's mouth and its stomach called?
16. How many sections does a bird's stomach have?
17. What do hummingbirds feed on?
18. What "R" is a large, flightless bird?

Birds are masters of the air. Their ability to fly enables them to travel long distances in search of food. Some migrate, flying thousands of miles each year to breed and take advantage of the abundance of food in the spring and the summer. All birds lay eggs with hard shells, and most make nests. Some birds sing in order to attract mates or to announce their territory.

intestine

crop

gizzard

Digestion 15 16
Most birds have a pouch between their mouth and stomach, known as the crop, that is used for storing food. A bird's stomach has two parts. The rear section is called the gizzard.

Feathers 2 5
Birds are the only animals in the world that have feathers. Feathers are what enable birds to fly. Feathers are lightweight but strong, made of many filaments held together by very small hooks.

Anatomy 1 8
A bird's body has several features to make it lighter, making flight less of an effort. For example, its bones are hollow and therefore lighter than those of other animals. Birds also have beaks instead of teeth.

rock dove slowing itself down as it lands

filaments

hooks

Flight 3
Most birds fly by flapping their wings, using them to push down on the air and lift their bodies upward. Some birds glide, holding out their wings and catching updrafts of air— this uses hardly any energy.

Wings 7
A bird's wings are like arms, with shoulder and elbow joints. Bones that formed fingers in birds' ancestors have adapted to form the ends of wings.

Large birds 4 6 18
The largest flying birds are pelicans (left), bustards, and swans. The largest bird of all is flightless—the ostrich. Other flightless giants include emus and rheas.

Plumage 9 11
The feathers that cover a bird are called plumage. Usually, male birds' plumage is colorful in order to attract mates, while females have dull plumage in order to conceal them when they're sitting on their eggs.

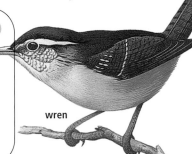

wren

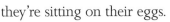

swallow

robin

greenfinch

kestrel

redshank

curlew

Beaks 10 13
A bird's beak is adapted for the food that it eats. The curlew's long beak is used for probing in the mud for worms, while the kestrel's hooked beak is used for tearing off meat.

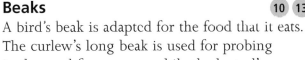

Hummingbirds 12 14 17
Hummingbirds feed on nectar from flowers and have long beaks and tongues to dip into the blossoms. These tiny birds flap their wings more than 70 times each second in order to hover (stay still in midair).

hummingbird

QUESTIONS:
African herbivores

Level 1

1. Do zebras have spots or stripes?
2. Are rhinos larger or smaller than rabbits?
3. Are zebras more closely related to horses or sheep?
4. Where on an elephant's body is its trunk?

Level 2

5. What is the world's largest land animal?
6. What is the world's tallest land animal?
7. What "B" is the word for a male elephant?
8. How can an elephant use its trunk to cool itself down?
9. African elephants can weigh more than one ton. True or false?
10. How tall do male giraffes grow: 10 ft. (3m), 20 ft. (6m), or 30 ft. (10m)?
11. Rhinos have excellent eyesight. True or false?
12. Do giraffes feed mostly on grass, insects, or leaves?
13. Which African predator can kill an elephant?
14. How many species (types) of zebras are there: three, five, or seven?

Level 3

15. What "P" hunts elephants for their tusks?
16. How many species (types) of rhinos are there?
17. What "J" is a species of rhino that lives in Asia?
18. What are elephants' tusks made of?

Herbivores are animals that eat plants but do not eat meat. Many of the world's largest herbivores live on the plains of Africa. There, there are vast amounts of grass and other vegetation for them to eat, so they exist in large numbers. Some herbivores live solitary lives, but most live in small groups or large herds.

Tough skin   13 15 18
Elephants' skin is thick and tough. This makes it difficult for predators to kill them, although sometimes lions do attack and kill elephants. Unfortunately, poachers also hunt elephants for their ivory tusks.

Elephants   5 7 9
The African elephant is the world's largest land animal. Adult male, or bull, elephants can weigh up to 12 tons.

Trunks   4 8
An elephant uses its trunk to spray water on itself to cool down and to pick things up. The trunk is formed from the nose and upper lip and contains thousands of muscles.

baby elephant spraying water from its trunk

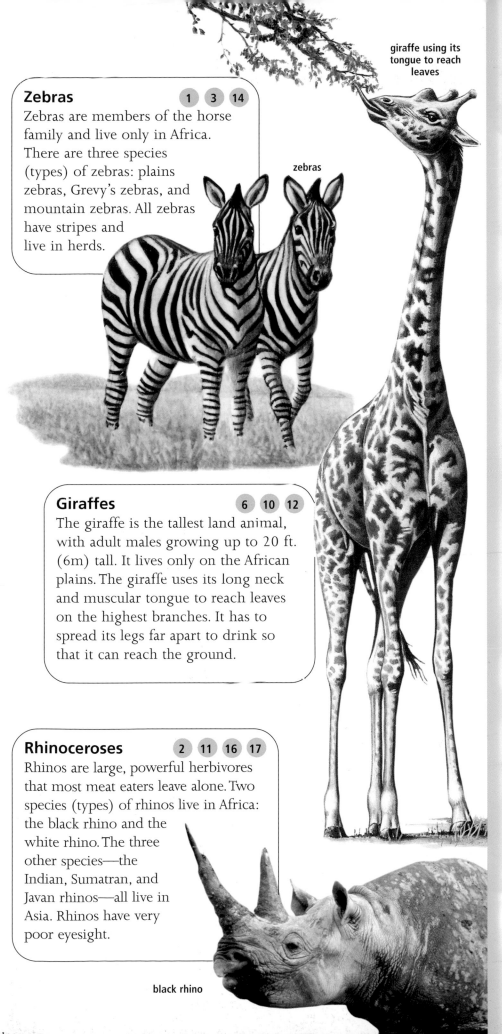

Zebras   1   3   14

Zebras are members of the horse family and live only in Africa. There are three species (types) of zebras: plains zebras, Grevy's zebras, and mountain zebras. All zebras have stripes and live in herds.

zebras

giraffe using its tongue to reach leaves

Giraffes   6   10   12

The giraffe is the tallest land animal, with adult males growing up to 20 ft. (6m) tall. It lives only on the African plains. The giraffe uses its long neck and muscular tongue to reach leaves on the highest branches. It has to spread its legs far apart to drink so that it can reach the ground.

Rhinoceroses   2   11   16   17

Rhinos are large, powerful herbivores that most meat eaters leave alone. Two species (types) of rhinos live in Africa: the black rhino and the white rhino. The three other species—the Indian, Sumatran, and Javan rhinos—all live in Asia. Rhinos have very poor eyesight.

black rhino

QUESTIONS:
Lions

Level 1

1. What is the name for a female lion?
2. RIP ED can be rearranged to give what name for a group of lions?
3. Which lions have manes: males or females?
4. Do male or female lions make up most of a pride?
5. Which are bigger: male or female lions?

Level 2

6. Which are the last members of a pride to feed at a kill?
7. Besides hunting, what do the lionesses do in the pride?
8. Which members of a pride of lions do most of the hunting?
9. Do female lions stay with or leave the pride when they grow up?
10. Do lions usually hunt in groups or alone?
11. Do lions ever fight to the death?
12. How long do lion cubs stay hidden from the rest of the pride: eight days, eight weeks, or eight months?
13. What do lion cubs have on their coats that adult lions do not?
14. How many male lions usually lead a pride?

Level 3

15. What is the name of the area in which a pride of lions lives and hunts?
16. What do lions use to mark the borders of their territory?
17. What do male lions do to keep other lions away?
18. How does a male lion take over a pride?

FIND THE ANSWER: Lions

The lion is sometimes called the "king of beasts." It is a large, majestic creature, the second biggest in the cat family after the tiger. Unlike most big cats, lions are social animals that live and hunt in groups called prides. Most of the world's wild lions live on the African plains, but a few live in northwest India in an area known as the Gir Forest.

Females   1 2 4 7 8 9
Female lions, called lionesses, make up most of a pride. They stay together throughout their lives. Daughters remain with their mother, aunts, and sisters even after they have grown up. As well as caring for the young, they do most of the hunting.

two males fighting

Territory   15 16
Each pride lives and hunts in an area of land known as its territory. The edges are patrolled and marked with urine, droppings, and scratch marks on trees.

Fighting   11 18
Rival males without prides may challenge another male for ownership of his pride. These fights can be violent and may even end in death.

lioness and her cub

Cubs   12 13
For the first eight weeks, lion cubs stay with their mother away from the pride. Unlike adult lions, lion cubs have spots, which gradually fade as they get older.

two lionesses hunting

Males   ③ ⑤ ⑭ ⑰

Male lions are much bigger than females and have a thick, shaggy mane. Each pride of lions is led by just one or, occasionally, two or three adult males, who mate with all of the females. Males roar to keep other lions away.

Hunting   ⑥ ⑩

Lionesses work together when hunting. When an animal is brought down, the kill is shared among the pride. Adult males feed first, followed by the lionesses, and, finally, the cubs.

male lion

QUESTIONS:
Polar animals

Level 1

1. Can penguins fly?
2. Can polar bears swim?
3. Polar bears can weigh more than one ton. True or false?
4. Do polar bears ever lie in wait for their prey?
5. Polar bears eat seals. True or false?

Level 2

6. In which season do migrating birds arrive in the polar regions?
7. Killer whales live in polar waters. True or false?
8. Why do some types of baby seals have white coats?
9. Do polar bears live close to the North Pole or the South Pole?
10. Penguins live in the Antarctic. True or false?
11. ALE BUG can be rearranged to give the name of which whale that lives in the Arctic waters?
12. Which sense do polar bears use to find most of their prey: sight, hearing, or smell?
13. How do penguins paddle through the water: with their wings or with their feet?
14. What is the world's largest type of penguin?

Level 3

15. Which bird flies all the way from the Antarctic to the Arctic and back again every year?
16. How can people protect baby seals from humans who hunt them for their fur?
17. Do narwhals live close to the North Pole or the South Pole?
18. What word is used for keeping an egg warm until it hatches?

FIND THE ANSWER: Polar animals

The regions around the poles are tough places to live. In order to survive, animals need to be able to cope with extreme cold and sometimes go for long periods without food. Weather conditions are harsh. In the middle of the winter, the sun never rises, and it is dark for weeks on end, while in the summer the sun is always in the sky—there are 24 hours of daylight.

Birds 6 15
Many birds migrate to the polar regions in the spring to lay their eggs. Every year Arctic terns fly all the way from the Antarctic to the Arctic and then back again. By leaving each pole just before the winter begins, they manage to completely avoid the coldest time of the year.

Polar bears 2 3 9
The polar bear is the world's largest land carnivore (meat eater). Adult males can weigh over one ton. Polar bears live in the Arctic, near the North Pole. Their large, padded feet act like paddles when swimming in the water.

Life in the water 7 11 17
Many polar animals live in the sea. Seals hunt fish under the ice. Other mammals in the polar seas include killer whales, which live both in the Arctic and Antarctic. Belugas and narwhals are small whales that live only in the Arctic waters.

Hunting 4 5 12
Polar bears hunt on the open ice and find most of their prey by smell. They sometimes feed on walrus but mostly on seals, chasing them when they are out of the water or lying in wait beside holes in the ice.

seal

polar bear

Penguins (1) (10) (13)

Penguins are flightless birds that live in the Antarctic. They are completely adapted to life in the sea. Their stiff wings act like paddles for their streamlined bodies.

penguins sliding on the ice

Winter wonder (14) (18)

Emperor penguins are the largest type of penguins. The males incubate (keep warm) the females' eggs by holding them on their feet throughout the winter.

male emperor penguin

baby penguin

Seal hunting (8) (16)

Some types of seals are born with beautiful white coats that hide them in the snow. Unfortunately, some people like to wear clothes made from this fur, and many seal pups are killed for this reason. People try to protect the baby seals by spraying them with a harmless dye, making their coats useless to the humans who hunt them.

spraying a ringed seal pup

QUESTIONS:
Farm animals

Level 1

1. Are dairy cows raised for their milk or their fur?
2. Is a rooster a male or a female chicken?
3. What animal do farmers raise to hunt for rats and mice?
4. Which farm animals produce wool?

Level 2

5. What "K" is a baby goat?
6. Today dairy cows are milked by hand. True or false?
7. On which part of a cow are its teats?
8. How many teats does a cow have?
9. Which have larger crests on their heads: male or female chickens?
10. Which animal is needed to make butter?
11. EAGER FERN can be rearranged to give the name of what type of chicken?
12. Which farm animal does pork come from?
13. What "L" is a meat from sheep?
14. What "F" is removed from a sheep by shearing it?

Level 3

15. What is the smallest piglet in a litter called?
16. How many teats does a goat have?
17. What type of dog is a border collie?
18. What is a male pig called?
19. What is the name for chickens that are kept in cages?

FIND THE ANSWER:  Farm animals

Some animals are cared for by people on farms. Most of them are raised to provide us with food, but some give us other useful products such as wool. Farm animals are domesticated versions of creatures that once lived in the wild. Most of the world's sheep, for example, are descended from the mouflon, which still lives in the wild in Europe and Asia.

rooster crowing at sunrise

Dairy cows   ① ⑥ ⑦ ⑩

Farmers raise dairy cows for their milk. Farmers used to milk by hand, but today machines gently squeeze the teats on the cows' udders to collect the milk. Milk can be used to make butter and cheese.

Roosters and hens   ② ⑨ ⑪ ⑲

Farmers raise chickens for eggs and meat. Male chickens (roosters) usually have bigger crests and longer tails than females (hens) and also crow at sunrise. Free-range chickens live outside in the open, while battery chickens are kept inside in cages.

milking a cow

Friesian cow

feed bucket

farmer

Cats   ③

Many farmers have cats to hunt mice and rats. Unlike most pet cats, farm cats spend their lives outside and sleep in barns and haystacks. Some farmers have dozens of cats.

Goats   ⑤ ⑧ ⑯

A female goat is called a nanny, and a male goat is a billy. Baby goats are known as kids. Goats' udders have two teats, unlike those of cows, which have four.

Southdown sheep

Hampshire Down sheep

Romney sheep

Scottish Blackface sheep

Sheep 4 13

Sheep are raised for their wool and also for their meat, which is known as mutton or lamb. Male sheep are called rams and usually have horns. Female sheep are known as ewes.

Sheep shearing 14

Once each year sheep have their wool cut off, a process known as shearing. The wool from one sheep is called a fleece. Sheep shearing is done by hand, using motorized clippers, and does not hurt the sheep at all.

border collie

Sheepdogs 17

Sheepdogs help farmers round up their sheep from the fields. Most of these dogs are intelligent and easy to train. One of the most common sheepdogs is the border collie. The Alsatian was originally bred as a sheepdog.

Pigs 12 15 18

Farmers raise pigs for their meat, which is known as pork, ham, or bacon. A male pig is called a boar, and a female is a sow. A sow may have ten or more piglets (baby pigs) in a litter. The smallest is called the runt.

mother sow with piglets

QUESTIONS:
Horses

Level 1

1. What are baby horses called?
2. What do cowboys wear to shade them from the sun?
3. In show jumping, do riders try to jump over obstacles or crash into them?
4. Horses are used to pull plows. True or false?
5. What "L" is the looped rope that cowboys use to catch cattle?
6. Are ponies larger or smaller than horses?

Level 2

7. Is an Exmoor a breed of pony or a breed of horse?
8. What is the largest breed of horse?
9. What is the main difference between the skeleton of a horse and the skeleton of a human?
10. When do male horses show their teeth and pull back their lips?
11. HEN CARS can be rearranged to give the name of what large farms where cowboys work?
12. What is worn by jumping horses to protect their ankles from knocks?
13. BANDY HURDS can be rearranged to give the name of what item used for removing dirt from a horse's coat?

Level 3

14. What "C" is a type of pony from Iran?
15. How does a horse show aggression?
16. What is the name of the bones that make up a horse's spine?
17. What type of brush is used to brush away loose hair on a horse?
18. What "D" is a horse-riding sport that tests obedience and rider control?

FIND THE ANSWER: Horses

People have raised horses for thousands of years. Before the invention of the car and train, they were the main form of transportation, carrying people on their backs or driving them in carts and carriages. Horses were also used by farmers to pull plows and by soldiers to carry them into battle. Today most horses are kept for pleasure, although some are still used as working animals.

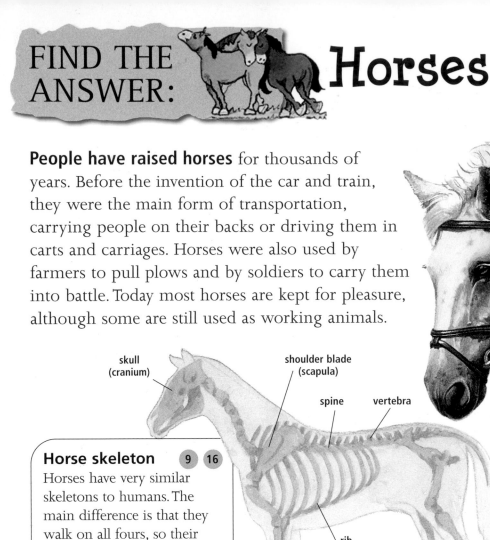

skull (cranium)

shoulder blade (scapula)

spine

vertebra

rib

radius

tibia

cannon bone

Horse skeleton 9 16

Horses have very similar skeletons to humans. The main difference is that they walk on all fours, so their front limbs are legs rather than arms. A horse's skeleton is based around its spine, which is made up of many bones known as vertebrae.

chestnut horse showing aggression

palomino male smelling a female

black horse

bay horse

Horse faces 10 15

Horses have different expressions. Ears held back show aggression. Males pull back their lips when they smell a female.

Training 1 12

Training begins when a horse is one year or more old and fully grown. Males are called stallions, females are mares, and baby horses are known as foals. If they are being trained for jumping, horses may wear bandages to protect their ankles from knocks.

rider

clearing a jump in show jumping

Show jumping 3 18

Show jumping is one of three horse-riding sports. The others are dressage, which tests obedience and rider control, and three-day eventing. In show jumping, a competitor has to ride the horse around a course with a series of different jumps.

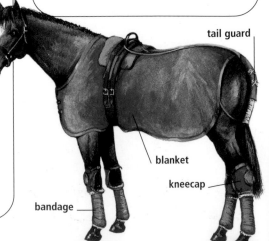

tail guard

blanket

kneecap

bandage

Cowboys 2 5 11

Cowboys ride horses to round up cattle. Today most work on ranches in the U.S., which are like large farms. Cowboys catch cattle with a lasso, a looped rope. They wear wide hats to shade them from the sun.

cowboy with lasso

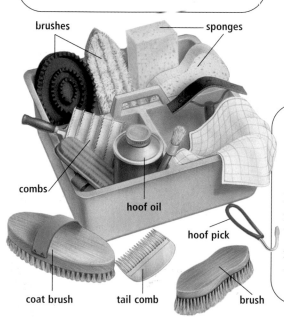

Working horses 4 8

Police on horseback are often used to control large crowds. Horses are also used to pull carts and plows in some places. The largest horse of all is the Shire horse, which can weigh one ton.

Ponies 6 7 14

Ponies are smaller breeds of horses. They are not as fast as large horses but are tougher and can live outside in all types of weather. Caspian ponies from Iran and Exmoor ponies from the U.K. live in the wild.

Shetland pony

brushes — sponges

combs

hoof oil

hoof pick

coat brush   tail comb   brush

Grooming 13 17

Owners like to keep their horses looking nice and clean by grooming them. Dandy brushes are used for removing dirt, currycombs brush away loose hair, and mane combs remove tangles in manes.

QUESTIONS:
Cats

Level 1

1. What are baby cats called?
2. Is catnip a type of plant or a type of animal?
3. Do cats creep up and pounce on their prey or chase it around and around until it is exhausted?
4. Do cat owners use brushes for grooming their cats or for feeding them?
5. Can cats climb?
6. Do young cats prefer playing with balls of string or with knitting needles?
7. Are cats good at jumping?

Level 2

8. Cats have claws. True or false?
9. What is a scratching post for?
10. Do cats prefer to live alone or in groups?
11. For how long do a cat's eyes stay closed after it is born?
12. How often should cats be fed?
13. Which fight more often: male cats or female cats?
14. What are male cats called?
15. Why is it a good idea to use a special dish to feed a cat?

Level 3

16. What part of a cat's body can be retracted (pulled back)?
17. From which animal are domestic cats descended?
18. Why do cats spray and mark things with their scent?

FIND THE ANSWER: Cats

Cats are popular household pets. Unlike dogs, they do not need to be walked every day, and they are usually happy to be left alone while their owners are at work. Today most people have cats as pets or companions, but in the past they were mostly kept to kill mice and other vermin that got into peoples' houses.

kittens

The cat's body ⑤ ⑦ ⑧ ⑯

Cats are muscular and flexible. They can jump long distances, and if they are dropped, they twist in the air and land on their feet. Cats are also good climbers. They have sharp claws, which they can retract (pull back into their paws) when not in use.

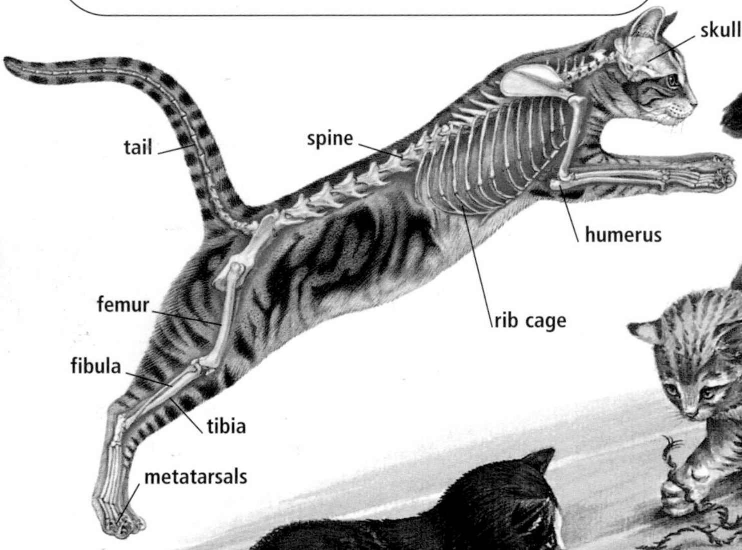

skull

tail

spine

humerus

femur

rib cage

fibula

tibia

metatarsals

Family ① ⑩ ⑪ ⑰

Cats are solitary animals. They are descended from the African wildcat, which lives mostly on its own. Female cats give birth to litters of several baby cats, known as kittens. Their eyes stay closed for the first week.

Cat accessories ② ④ ⑨

Cats like to keep their claws sharp by scratching on a scratching post. They also like to play with toys and are fond of catnip, a plant. Owners use brushes to groom their cats and shampoo to wash them.

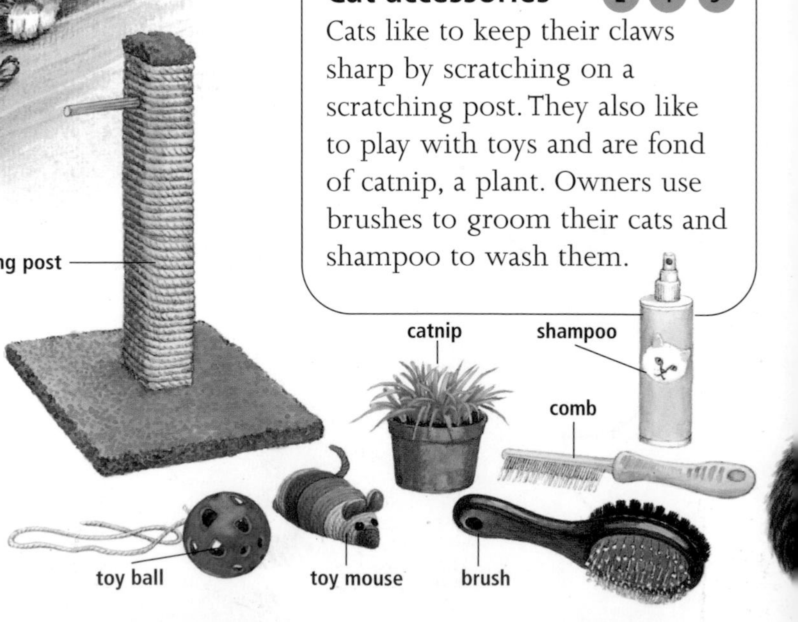

scratching post

catnip

shampoo

comb

Learning ③ ⑥

Kittens enjoy playing with many objects and are fond of balls of string. Playing helps them learn and get used to how their bodies work. As they play, they learn how to hunt, creeping up on their toys before pouncing.

toy ball

toy mouse

brush

Feeding ⑫ ⑮

Cats should be fed at least once a day, either with dry food or wet food from cans or pouches. It is a good idea to put a cat's food in a special dish. Cats learn to associate the dish with feeding and come running when their owners approach them.

moist food

Territory ⑬ ⑭ ⑱

Both wild and domestic cats defend their home areas, or territories, from others. Male cats, or tomcats, in particular, will fight others that enter their area. Cats spray and mark their territory as a warning to stay away.

defensive cat

scent marking

cats fighting

QUESTIONS:
Dogs

Level 1

1. What is a baby dog called?
2. Are most police dogs Alsatians or Dalmatians?
3. Were pit bulls originally bred for fighting or bringing slippers?
4. Are most Labradors friendly or aggressive?
5. The terrier is the largest breed of dog. True or false?

Level 2

6. What is a group of related puppies called?
7. How long does it take for a puppy to grow into an adult: six months, one year, or three years?
8. Which "S" is a type of dog that is often trained to be a sniffer dog?
9. How might a hearing dog help a deaf owner?
10. If a dog wags its tail, is it happy or angry?
11. Does a sad dog drop its tail or raise it?
12. Which wild animal is the ancestor of all domestic dogs?
13. EDGIER REVEL TORN can be rearranged to spell what breed of dog, often trained as a guide dog?
14. Which would make a better guard dog: a Rottweiler or a Labrador?

Level 3

15. How long should you wait before giving away puppies to new owners?
16. During which year of a dog's life is it easiest to train?
17. What is another word for cutting off a dog's tail?
18. How can you tell when a dog is frightened?
19. What type of dog was bred to hunt large animals?

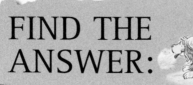

Dogs

People say that a dog is a man's best friend, and most dog owners agree that this is true. Dogs are friendly, protective, and loyal companions. They are descended from wolves, which are pack-living animals, so a dog thinks of its owners as members of its pack. Unlike wolves, most dogs have been bred to be less aggressive and more friendly to humans.

Puppies 1 6 15

A baby dog is called a puppy. Female dogs have a litter of several puppies at a time. Many people sell their dog's puppies to new owners. They have to wait until the puppies are a few weeks old and big enough to be away from their mother.

mother and litter

Growing up 7 16

Puppies take around one year to grow up into adults. This first year is the best time to train them, as their brains develop. (Adult dogs need more time for training.) Puppies are playful and enjoy wrestling.

adult golden Labrador

Learning 2 8

You can train dogs to do many things. Some Alsatians are trained to catch criminals, and spaniels are trained as sniffer dogs to find illegal drugs. You can train a pet dog to make it easier to control, using food treats as a reward.

Tails 10 11 17 18

A dog's tail may be straight or curly. A happy dog wags its tail, and a sad dog drops it. A confident dog holds its tail up high, while a frightened dog holds its tail between its legs. On some breeds the tails may be cut off (docked) when they are puppies.

frightened dog

docked tail

sad dog

curly tail

Dog breeds ⑤ ⑫ ⑲

All dogs are descended from wolves, but over the years many breeds have been created. Dog breeds are grouped by characteristics. Terriers, for example, are small dogs that were originally bred to hunt rodents. Hounds were bred to hunt larger animals.

Guide dogs ⑨ ⑬

Golden retrievers and black Labradors are trained as guide dogs for blind people. They look out for obstacles on the street. Some dogs are trained as hearing dogs, alerting a deaf owner if there is a knock at the door, for example.

Temperament ③ ④ ⑭

Dog breeds have different temperaments. Labradors are friendly and eager to please, making them perfect pets. Pit bulls and Rottweilers were bred to fight, so they make better guard dogs.

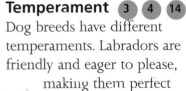

confident dog

straight tail

happy dog

wolf

Alsatian

collie

basenji

basset hound

Dalmatian

bulldog

fox terrier

QUESTIONS:
Where in the world?

Level 1
1. Would you find a European bison in Poland or in Madagascar?
2. Do tigers live in Europe or Asia?
3. TAIPAN DANG can be rearranged to give the name of which animal that lives in the bamboo forests of China?

Level 2
4. Are tamarins types of monkeys or turtles?
5. Which island off Africa is home to all of the world's lemurs?
6. Where in the world does the numbat live?
7. Which country is home to the Iberian lynx?

Level 3
8. What is the world's largest tree-living animal?
9. The Tasmanian tiger is another name for which animal?
10. What is the name of the largest bird in North America?

Where in the world?

In many parts of the world, many species of animals have been disappearing at an alarming rate. Some have been hunted close to extinction by humans, while others are threatened by damage to their natural habitats or by climate change. Endangered species include not only large mammals, such as the Asian elephant, but also countless birds, fish, and insects.

Asia 2 3 8
Asia has many unique species, including many that are endangered such as giant pandas, tigers, gibbons, and orangutans, the world's largest tree-living animals.

North America 10
The California condor, North America's largest bird, is in danger of extinction. In 2002 there were only 200 left—all in captivity.

Europe 1 7
Endangered species include the European bison, which lives in Poland and the far west of Russia, and the Iberian lynx, which is found only in Spain.

NORTH AMERICA

EUROPE

ASIA

AFRICA

SOUTH AMERICA

AUSTRALASIA

Africa 5
The island of Madagascar, off the east coast of Africa, is home to the endangered species of primates called lemurs.

South America
The golden lion tamarin, a small monkey, is native to the coastal forests of Brazil and is one of the world's rarest animals.

Australia 6 9
The thylacine, or Tasmanian tiger, is now thought to be extinct. Other endangered species include the numbat, the northern hairy-nosed wombat, and the Australian sea lion.

Answers 1) Poland **2)** Asia **3)** Giant panda **4)** Monkeys **5)** Madagascar **6)** Australia **7)** Spain **8)** The orangutan **9)** The thylacine **10)** The California condor

QUIZ TWO
Geography

Continents

International community

Flags

Natural wonders

Coasts

Rivers

Deserts

The poles

Continents

Level 1

1. Where is the Nile river?
2. Which continent lies to the east of Europe?
3. Is Asia the second-most-populated continent?
4. Is Central America part of North America or South America?
5. What is the smallest continent?

Level 2

6. What is the world's largest country?
7. What divides Europe from Africa?
8. What population milestone was reached in 1802?
9. Is Sydney the capital of Australia?
10. In which continent would you find the world's highest mountains?
11. What larger landmass encompasses Europe?
12. How many billion people did the world's population reach in 1999: one, five, six, or 11?
13. Are the Andes mountains on the east or west coast of South America?

Level 3

14. How much of the Amazon rain forest lies outside of Brazil?
15. What are the names of the island groups of Australasia?
16. By how many million people per year was the world's population increasing in 2004?
17. How many countries are in Africa: 47, 52, or 53?
18. In which continent is the world's largest freshwater lake?
19. How long is the Andes mountain range?

FIND THE ANSWER: Continents

Millions of years ago, the world's land was all connected in one "supercontinent." Over time the land shifted and settled into the seven continents that we know today. This process is known as continental drift. Antarctica is the world's only unpopulated continent because 98 percent of its land is covered in ice. It is also the coldest, windiest, and driest continent.

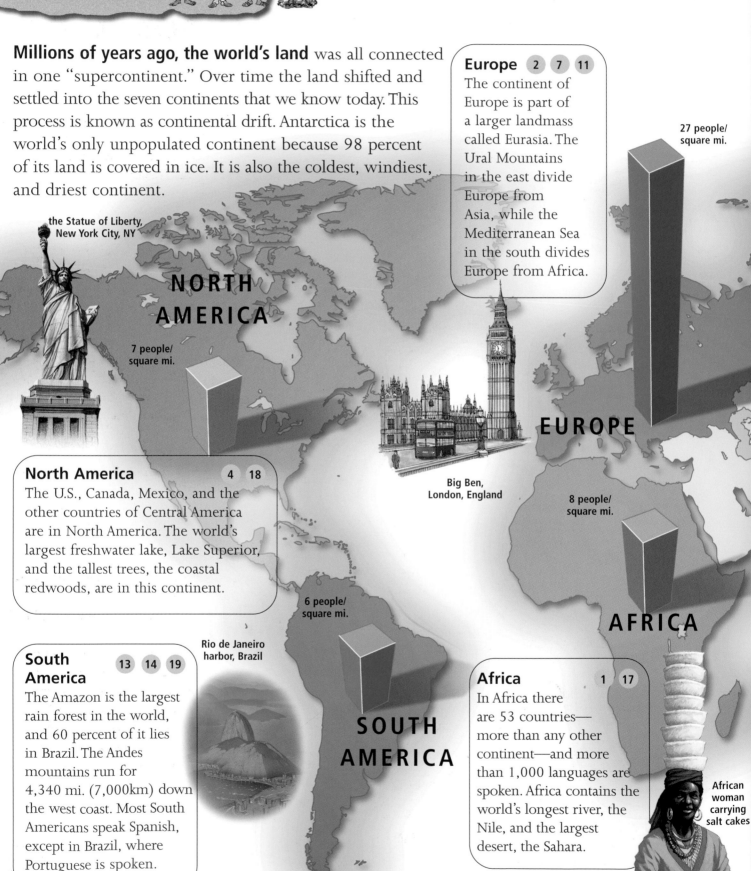

the Statue of Liberty, New York City, NY

Europe 2 7 11
The continent of Europe is part of a larger landmass called Eurasia. The Ural Mountains in the east divide Europe from Asia, while the Mediterranean Sea in the south divides Europe from Africa.

27 people/ square mi.

NORTH AMERICA

7 people/ square mi.

Big Ben, London, England

EUROPE

8 people/ square mi.

North America 4 18
The U.S., Canada, Mexico, and the other countries of Central America are in North America. The world's largest freshwater lake, Lake Superior, and the tallest trees, the coastal redwoods, are in this continent.

6 people/ square mi.

Rio de Janeiro harbor, Brazil

AFRICA

South America 13 14 19
The Amazon is the largest rain forest in the world, and 60 percent of it lies in Brazil. The Andes mountains run for 4,340 mi. (7,000km) down the west coast. Most South Americans speak Spanish, except in Brazil, where Portuguese is spoken.

SOUTH AMERICA

Africa 1 17
In Africa there are 53 countries—more than any other continent—and more than 1,000 languages are spoken. Africa contains the world's longest river, the Nile, and the largest desert, the Sahara.

African woman carrying salt cakes

Population increase (8) (12) (16)

The world population has grown at an increasingly fast rate, even though birth rates have gone down in many countries. In 1802 the population reached one billion people, and by 1999 it had reached six billion. By 2004, the population increase was 75 million per year.

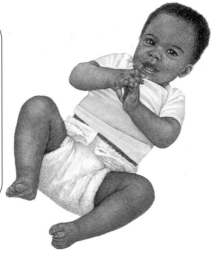

30 people/ square mi.

ASIA

Asia (3) (6) (10)

Asia is the largest continent and the most populated. It contains the world's largest country, the Russian Federation, as well as the Middle Eastern countries, the Far East, and India. The world's highest mountains are in Asia, including 96 in the Himalayas.

a rickshaw, China

Australasia (5) (9) (15)

The smallest continent includes Australia, New Zealand, Papua New Guinea, and the island groups of the south Pacific: Melanesia, Micronesia, and Polynesia. Sydney is Australia's largest city, and Canberra is its capital.

AUSTRALASIA

1 person/ square mi.

the Sydney Opera House, Australia

QUESTIONS:
International community

Level 1

1. The United Nations was formed during World War I. True or false?
2. What does NATO stand for: the North Atlantic Treaty Organization or the North Antarctic Treaty Organization?
3. All peacekeeping units are armed. True or false?
4. What is the single currency of the European Union?
5. CRESS ROD can be rearranged to give the name of what organization that provides medical aid?

Level 2

6. Why was NATO formed?
7. What convention protects wounded soldiers and prisoners?
8. In what city is the UN headquarters?
9. How many countries are in the UN?
10. What treaty marked the beginning of the European Union?
11. In what building do member nations of the UN meet?
12. For what purpose can peacekeeping units use their weapons?

Level 3

13. In what year did the UN headquarters officially open?
14. What treaty led to the formation of the European Union?
15. What is the full name of the Red Cross?
16. How much money was donated to buy land for the UN headquarters?
17. What is the name of the central command of NATO's military forces?
18. Who first used the term "United Nations"?

International community

The countries of the world have formed many organizations in order to help each other. These groups provide medical and military aid, as well as opportunities for trade. Many international committees try to make the world into a safer, more peaceful place.

the UN flag

United Nations ① ⑨ ⑱

The term "United Nations" (UN) was first used by U.S. President Franklin D. Roosevelt during World War II, but the UN was not officially established until 1945. Since then, it has grown from its original 51 members to 191.

Peacekeeping ③ ⑫

When armed fighting breaks out within countries, UN peacekeeping groups may be called in to help. They may set up refugee camps and help maintain law and order. There are armed and unarmed UN groups. Armed groups are only allowed to use their weapons for self-defense.

Headquarters ⑧ ⑪ ⑬ ⑯

The UN headquarters officially opened on January 9, 1951 on the banks of the East river in New York City. An American millionaire named John D. Rockefeller Jr. donated $8.5 million to buy the land. Member nations meet in the General Assembly building.

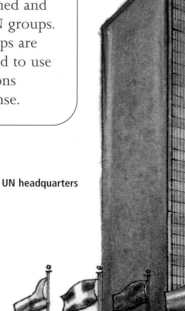

UN headquarters

flags of UN member states

European Union headquarters

European Union 4 10 14

The Treaty of Paris, in 1951, marked the beginning of the European Union (EU). The European Community (EC) grew out of this, and the Maastricht Treaty, signed in 1992, led to the formation of the EU and the single European currency, the euro.

5 euro bill

NATO 2 6 17

The North Atlantic Treaty Organization (NATO) was formed in 1949 to keep peace in its 26 member states. They all help each other if any of their states is attacked. Supreme Headquarters Allied Powers Europe (SHAPE) is the central command of NATO's military forces.

Red Cross 5 7 15

The International Committee of the Red Cross and the Red Crescent Movement provides medical aid in war and peace. The Geneva Convention also helps protect wounded soldiers and prisoners.

QUESTIONS:
Flags

Level 1

1. What colors could a pirate flag be?
2. Where are navy flags used: at sea or in space?
3. In what type of sport is a black-and-white checkered flag used?
4. What type of flag do explorers place on lands that they have discovered?
5. Which has the oldest national flag: Scotland or the United States?

Level 2

6. Which sport uses flags: football, cycling, or rowing?
7. What are navy flags called?
8. What event prompted the French flag to be redesigned?
9. Are signaling flags used alone or together?
10. What is semaphore?
11. How many U.S. flags have been placed on the Moon: four, five, or six?
12. Which color is not used in navy flags: yellow, black, or green?

Level 3

13. What do referees use flags to indicate in a football game?
14. In semaphore, how is an "R" signaled?
15. On a pirate flag, what does an hourglass symbolize?
16. What color flags are used in semaphore?
17. In which century were pirate flags first used?
18. What displayed a U.S. flag on Mars?

FIND THE ANSWER:  Flags

Flags have been used for centuries both as identification and to communicate messages. In the Middle Ages, for example, they were used in battle to identify leaders. Flags vary greatly in color and style, but they all convey an immediate visual message.

China

Brazil

Sweden

Greece

Germany

Israel

National flags (5) (8)
National flags are used to identify individual countries. Scotland has the oldest national flag. Sometimes countries change their flags: the French flag was redesigned as the famous tricolor flag in 1794 after the revolution.

Sports flags (3) (6) (13)
Flags are used in many sports, including rugby, rowing, and cycling to communicate with the athletes. Referees use flags in football games to indicate a penalty. A checkered flag is used in car and motorcycle racing to signal the end of a race.

checkered flag

Navy flags (2) (7) (9) (12)
Ships at sea communicate with navy flags called signaling flags. These convey different meanings when used alone or together. They use colors that can be seen at sea: blue, white, red, black, and yellow.

Semaphore (10) (14) (16)
One signaling system, semaphore, uses two square red-and-yellow flags held in different positions to indicate letters. Arms and flags straight out mean "R".

signaling flags

Sudan

Australia

United Kingdom

Canada

Argentina

Turkey

South Korea

Jamaica

Austria

Pirate flags

 1 15 17

A red or black pirate flag was supposed to frighten, with images such as a skull, meaning death, or an hourglass, meaning that time was running out. These flags were used by British pirates from around 1700.

Black Bart's flag

Christopher Moody's flag

Calico Jack's flag

Explorers' flags 4 11 18

Explorers often plant their national flag on the lands that they discover. Six U.S. flags have been placed on the Moon. Each U.S. space shuttle is given its own flag. The *Viking* lander displayed a U.S. flag as it explored Mars.

U.S. flag on the Moon

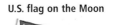

QUESTIONS:
Natural wonders

Level 1

1. What is the tallest mountain in the world?
2. What is the tallest waterfall in the world?
3. K2 is in Europe. True or false?
4. The Great Barrier Reef lies off the coast of which country?
5. The Great Barrier Reef can be seen from space. True or false?
6. Which is longer: the Grand Canyon or the Great Barrier Reef?

Level 2

7. Who were the first people to reach the top of Mount Everest?
8. How is the length of the Grand Canyon measured?
9. How many times higher is Angel Falls than Niagara Falls: ten, 15, or 20?
10. What is the Hillary Step?
11. How old are the rocks in the Grand Canyon?
12. In what continent is the widest waterfall in the world?
13. What is another name for *aurora borealis*?

Level 3

14. What causes the northern lights?
15. How much older are the Alps than the Himalayas?
16. How high is Mount Everest?
17. What is the Latin name of the southern lights?
18. What geographical feature is 35,368 ft. (10,783m) wide?

FIND THE ANSWER:  Natural wonders

Spectacular natural features are found all over the world and include amazing waterfalls, fiery volcanoes, and natural phenomena such as the northern lights. Wind and water erosion have created some of these features, such as canyons, while the movement of Earth's plates has created others such as the world's highest mountains.

oxygen cylinders

Mount Everest 1 3 15 16
Mount Everest, the tallest mountain in the world, is part of the Himalayan mountain range in Asia. Its peak is 29,000 ft. (8,850m) high. The second-highest mountain, K2, is also in the Himalayas. The Himalayas are 60 million years old—younger than the Alps in Europe, which formed 75 million years ago.

Conquering Everest 7 10
In 1953 New Zealander Edmund Hillary and Nepali Tenzing Norgay became the first people to reach the peak of Mount Everest. A steep section of the mountain has since been named Hillary Step.

angelfish

staghorn coral

harlequin tusk fish

jack fish

hard coral

Coral reefs 4 5 6
The Great Barrier Reef off the coast of Australia, is more than 1,200 mi. (2,000km) long and is visible from outer space. More than 5,000 species of plants and animals live there.

fan coral

Victoria Falls, Africa

Waterfalls ② ⑨ ⑫ ⑱

Angel Falls in South America is the tallest waterfall in the world at 3,211 ft. (979m) high. It is 15 times higher than Niagara Falls in North America. The widest waterfall is Khone Falls in Asia. It is 35,368 ft. (10,783m) wide.

Auroras ⑬ ⑭ ⑰

The northern lights (*aurora borealis*) and the southern lights (*aurora australis*) are dancing displays of colored lights in the night sky. Auroras are caused by high-speed particles from the Sun colliding with gas molecules to create light.

Canyons ⑥ ⑧ ⑪

The Grand Canyon, in Arizona, is the largest canyon in the world. It is 277 mi. (446km) long and almost 5,000 ft. (1,500m) deep. The canyon's length is measured by the Colorado river that cuts through it. The oldest rocks there are two billion years old, though the canyon itself is probably only around five or six million years old.

the Grand Canyon, Arizona

QUESTIONS:
Coasts

Level 1

1. A tsunami is caused by the wind. True or false?
2. ACE VASE can be rearranged to give what name for a cavern in a cliff?
3. What is the wearing down of a headland called: erosion or erasure?
4. What two materials do waves deposit on beaches?
5. What "W" causes waves?
6. HELLO BOW can be rearranged to give the name of what coastal feature?

Level 2

7. What is special about the Painted Cave?
8. What does the word "tsunami" mean?
9. What causes water to gush through a blowhole?
10. The fetch is the material deposited on a beach. True or false?
11. A stack is a mound of sand. True or false?
12. Is seawater acidic or alkaline?

Level 3

13. Which is formed first: a cave or a blowhole?
14. How fast do tsunami waves move?
15. What coastal process do groins prevent?
16. On what island is the Painted Cave?
17. How high can tsunamis be?
18. A stack is formed from which coastal feature?

FIND THE ANSWER: Coasts

The world's coastlines are around 312,000 mi. (504,000km) long, which is long enough to circle the globe 12 times. Primary coasts are formed by changes in the land such as river deltas. Many of these coastlines were formed as the sea levels changed over thousands of years. Secondary coasts are formed by changes in the ocean such as coral reefs.

Coastal erosion   (3) (12)
Coastlines do not stay the same. They change continually as they are worn down by water washing pebbles and rocks against the shore, a process called erosion. Seawater is also acidic, helping wear down coastlines.

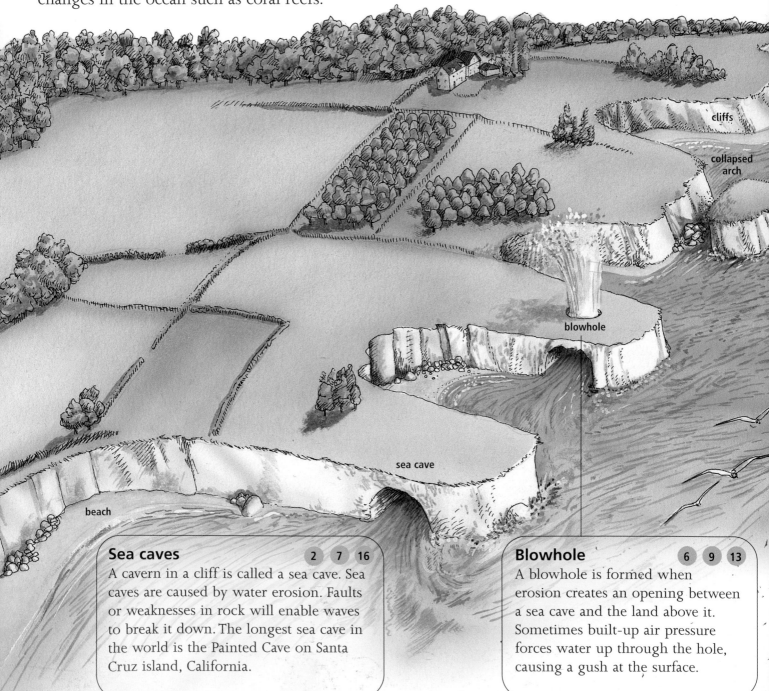

cliffs

collapsed arch

blowhole

sea cave

beach

Sea caves   (2) (7) (16)
A cavern in a cliff is called a sea cave. Sea caves are caused by water erosion. Faults or weaknesses in rock will enable waves to break it down. The longest sea cave in the world is the Painted Cave on Santa Cruz island, California.

Blowhole   (6) (9) (13)
A blowhole is formed when erosion creates an opening between a sea cave and the land above it. Sometimes built-up air pressure forces water up through the hole, causing a gush at the surface.

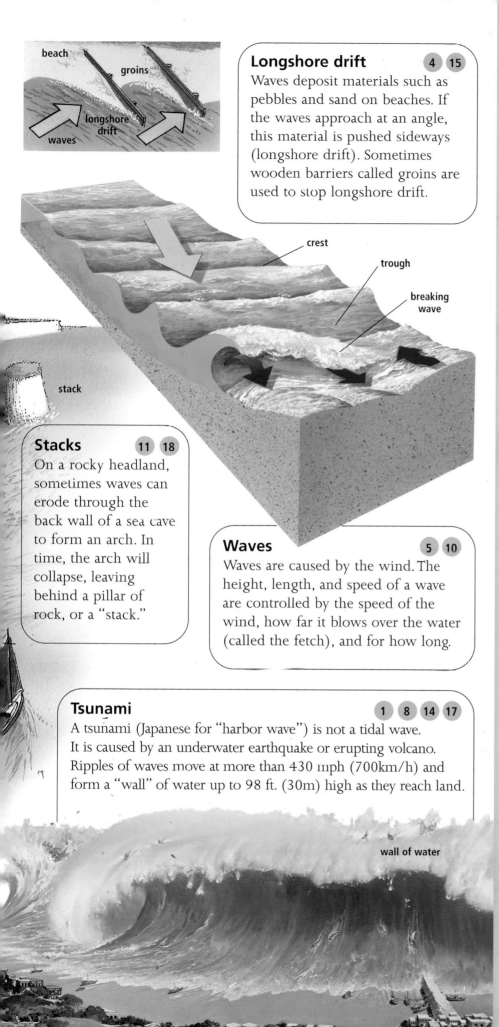

Longshore drift (4) (15)

Waves deposit materials such as pebbles and sand on beaches. If the waves approach at an angle, this material is pushed sideways (longshore drift). Sometimes wooden barriers called groins are used to stop longshore drift.

beach
groins
longshore drift
waves

crest
trough
breaking wave
stack

Stacks (11) (18)

On a rocky headland, sometimes waves can erode through the back wall of a sea cave to form an arch. In time, the arch will collapse, leaving behind a pillar of rock, or a "stack."

Waves (5) (10)

Waves are caused by the wind. The height, length, and speed of a wave are controlled by the speed of the wind, how far it blows over the water (called the fetch), and for how long.

Tsunami (1) (8) (14) (17)

A tsunami (Japanese for "harbor wave") is not a tidal wave. It is caused by an underwater earthquake or erupting volcano. Ripples of waves move at more than 430 mph (700km/h) and form a "wall" of water up to 98 ft. (30m) high as they reach land.

wall of water

QUESTIONS:
Rivers

Level 1

1. What is the beginning of a river called?
2. In what continent are the Great Lakes?
3. Do waterfalls flow over a ledge of hard or soft rock?
4. What is the name of the process by which water moves between the land and sea and back again?
5. What is the name of the area of flat land on both sides of a river?

Level 2

6. What "R" is precipitation?
7. What type of lakes are created by ice sheets?
8. What is formed when a river floods shallow lakes or ponds?
9. Do tributaries increase or decrease the water volume of a river?
10. What happens to evaporated water?
11. What other name is used for an estuary?
12. Headwaters are the top of a waterfall. True or false?
13. What prevents water seepage in a marshland?
14. What forms at the bottom of a waterfall?

Level 3

15. What "Y" is a waterfall in the U.S., created by a glacier?
16. What name is given to fertile land formed on a floodplain?
17. What can form from sediment in an estuary?
18. How was Lake Tanganyika formed?

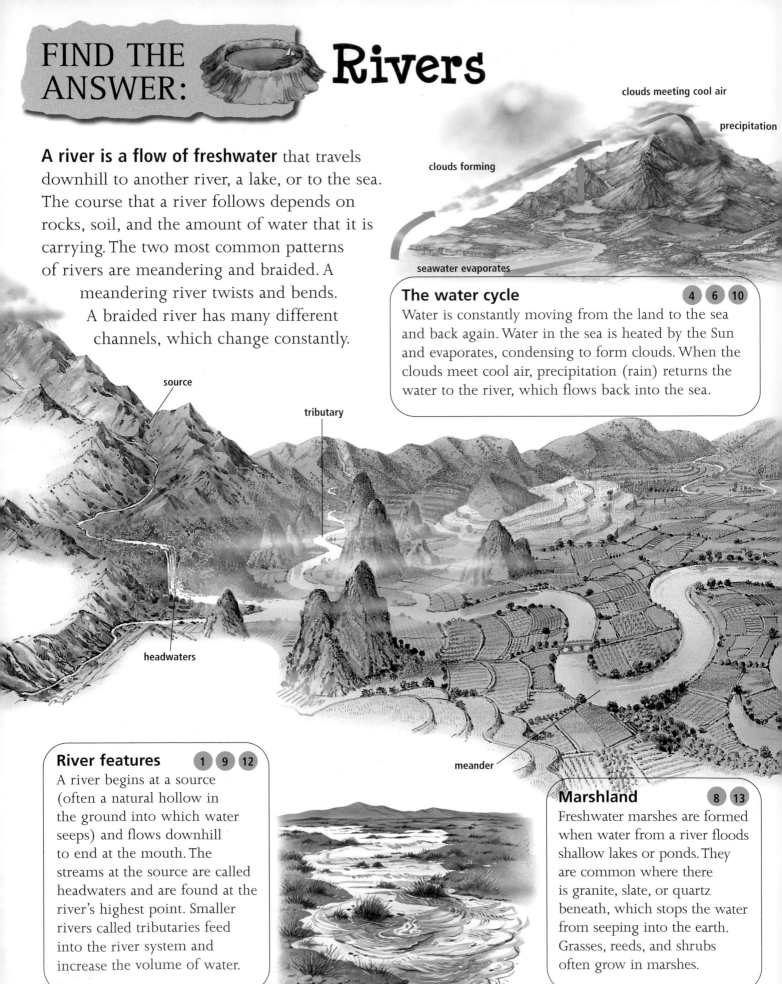

Rivers

A river is a flow of freshwater that travels downhill to another river, a lake, or to the sea. The course that a river follows depends on rocks, soil, and the amount of water that it is carrying. The two most common patterns of rivers are meandering and braided. A meandering river twists and bends. A braided river has many different channels, which change constantly.

clouds meeting cool air

precipitation

clouds forming

seawater evaporates

The water cycle   4 6 10

Water is constantly moving from the land to the sea and back again. Water in the sea is heated by the Sun and evaporates, condensing to form clouds. When the clouds meet cool air, precipitation (rain) returns the water to the river, which flows back into the sea.

source

tributary

headwaters

meander

River features   1 9 12

A river begins at a source (often a natural hollow in the ground into which water seeps) and flows downhill to end at the mouth. The streams at the source are called headwaters and are found at the river's highest point. Smaller rivers called tributaries feed into the river system and increase the volume of water.

Marshland   8 13

Freshwater marshes are formed when water from a river floods shallow lakes or ponds. They are common where there is granite, slate, or quartz beneath, which stops the water from seeping into the earth. Grasses, reeds, and shrubs often grow in marshes.

Waterfalls 3 14 15

Most waterfalls form where an area of soft rock lies in front of an area of hard rock (stage one). The soft rock is quickly worn away by the river, leaving a ledge of hard rock over which the water falls (stage two). The gushing water creates a plunge pool at the bottom (stage three). Other waterfalls, such as Yosemite Falls in California, were made by glaciers.

stage one

hard rock   soft rock

stage two

soft rock worn away

stage three

plunge pool

Lakes 2 7 18

Freshwater lakes, such as the Great Lakes in North America, are formed by glaciers or ice sheets. Other lakes, such as Lake Tanganyika in Africa, are made by Earth fault movements.

Floodplains 5 16

Flat land alongside a river is called a floodplain. If the river overflows, it deposits sand and mud on the land. As the water drains away, this sediment forms fertile land known as alluvium.

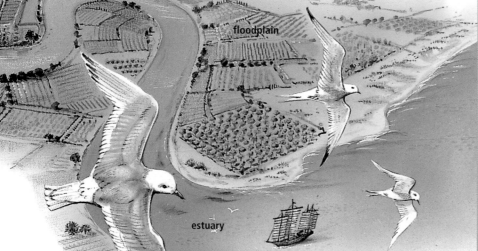

lake

floodplain

estuary

Estuary 11 17

A river mixes with salty water from the sea to form an estuary, or harbor. A delta may form from sediment in the river.

QUESTIONS:
Deserts

Level 1
1. What "D" is a sandy desert feature?
2. Which animal is used to carry people and goods in the desert?
3. Sand holds water. True or false?
4. What plant with spines can survive in a desert?
5. What "B" is the home of a meerkat?

Level 2
6. Is a Tuareg a type of sand dune or a member of a desert tribe?
7. What type of sand dune forms when the wind blows in all directions?
8. What is a one-humped camel called?
9. What is the name for wind carrying away fine sand?
10. What is the slope of a sand dune called?
11. Wind blowing in two different directions creates which type of sand dune?
12. Is a hoodoo: a type of sand dune, a rock formation, or a desert rodent?
13. In which desert would you find a Tuareg?

Level 3
14. What desert plant can be more than 200 years old?
15. What "F" is a type of fox that lives in the desert?
16. What is a barchan?
17. What substance is formed by cemented sand and gravel?
18. What features of a camel help it survive in deserts?

Deserts

hoodoo rock

Deserts are dry areas of land with little rainfall or plant and animal life. The driest desert in the world is the Atacama Desert in Chile, South America. Deserts may be hot, such as the Sahara in Africa, or cold such as the Antarctic. Hot deserts can be cold at night because rocks lose their heat quickly, and there is little humidity or vegetation to hold in heat.

Desert winds 9 12
The wind wears away rocks in deserts by deflation (carrying away fine sand) and abrasion (friction). These processes create arches, ridges, flat-topped mesas, and pedestal rocks. They also create formations called hoodoo rocks, which look like giant mushrooms.

Nomads 6 13
Nomads are people who move from place to place. The nomadic Tuareg tribe lives in the Sahara desert in Africa.

dromedary camel

Tuareg tribesman

Desert animals 5 15
Many desert animals, such as the fennec fox, are nocturnal (active at night). Others, such as the meerkat, live in burrows to keep themselves cool.

Caravans 2 8 18
The Tuaregs use "caravans" of camels to carry people and goods. Dromedary (one-humped) camels can go without water for days. Their thick, padded feet can walk on hot sand without feeling pain.

barchan

linear

star

Types of sand dunes

A curved barchan dune forms when the wind blows in one direction. A star dune forms when the wind blows in all directions. A linear dune is formed when the wind blows in two different directions.

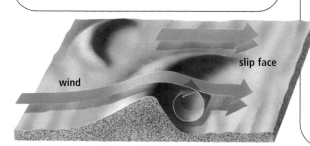

wind

slip face

Sand dune formation

Dunes, or large piles of sand, form as desert sand is moved and shifted by wind until it creates a slope, called a slip face. A dune's shape depends on the wind speed and direction. Sometimes sand dunes migrate, blown along by wind.

Soil

In deserts water seeps through sand but can be trapped by soil and rocks. Hard layers of cemented sand and gravel (calcrete) are found in many deserts.

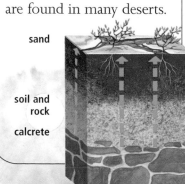

sand

soil and rock

calcrete

Saguaro cactus

Cacti

Found in the deserts of North and South America, cacti are succulent plants that store water in their stems and branches in order to survive. Most cacti have spines instead of leaves. The Saguaro cactus can live for 200 years and grow to 40 ft. (12m) tall.

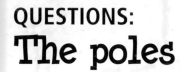

QUESTIONS:
The poles

Level 1
1. On which continent is the South Pole?
2. The explorer Robert Scott reached the South Pole. True or false?
3. LIE CRAG can be rearranged to give the name of what polar feature?
4. Icebergs are lumps of ice that have broken away from glaciers. True or false?

Level 2
5. What is a hollow formed by melting blocks of ice called: a kettle hole or a sinkhole?
6. How much of an iceberg is visible above the waterline?
7. Who was the first person to reach the South Pole?
8. Why do glaciers shift?
9. Today most Inuit use dogsleds to travel over the Arctic ice. True or false?
10. What imaginary line runs between the two poles?
11. What is a moraine?
12. What language is spoken by the Inuit?
13. What "P" is an item of clothing worn by Arctic people?

Level 3
14. Do the Inuit live close to the North Pole or the South Pole?
15. In which year did a person reach the South Pole for the first time?
16. Near which pole are flat-topped tabular icebergs found?
17. How far would Robert Scott and his crew have had to travel to safety on the South Pole?
18. What Arctic people live in Greenland?

FIND THE ANSWER:  The poles

The extreme north and south points of the world are called the poles. The polar regions of the Arctic in the north and Antarctica in the south are the coldest places on Earth. At the poles themselves, the sun never sets for months in the summer, while in the winter there is complete darkness for several months.

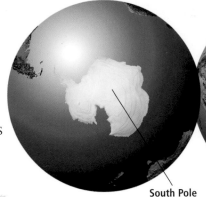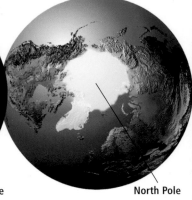

South Pole

North Pole

Native peoples 12 14 18
The Inuit people live in the Arctic regions of Siberia, Alaska, Canada, and Greenland. They speak Inuktitut. Other native groups include the Kalaalit of Greenland and the Yupik of the Russian Federation.

North and South 1 10
The axis on which Earth turns runs between the North and South Poles. The North Pole is on the frozen seas of the Arctic Ocean. The South Pole is on the continent of Antarctica.

Living in the Arctic 9 13
Arctic people were originally migrating hunters and fishermen, but most now live in modern communities. Parkas made of animal skin provided warmth, and dogsleds were used to travel across the ice. Snowmobiles are now used.

Scott 2 7 15 17
Robert Falcon Scott tried to become the first person to reach the South Pole. He got there on January 17, 1912, but Norwegian Roald Amundsen had already reached it on December 14, 1911. Scott and his crew starved to death in Antarctica, around 10.5 mi. (17km) away from the supply depot.

traditional-style parka

dogsled

glacier

Glaciers   3   5   8   11

Glaciers are formed when fallen snow packs together over many years and crystallizes into ice. Most glaciers are found in mountainous or polar regions. Glaciers shift over time due to the weight of the ice and gravity. A melting glacier may leave behind ridges of rock called moraines. Blocks of ice that melt may form a hollow called a kettle hole.

castle iceberg

Icebergs   4   6   16

Icebergs are lumps of floating ice that break away from glaciers in a process called calving. Nine tenths of an iceberg is below water. Pinnacle, or castle, icebergs form in the Arctic. Flat-topped tabular icebergs form in Antarctica.

QUESTIONS:
Where in the world?

Level 1

1. What city is nicknamed "The Big Apple"?
2. In which country is Rio de Janeiro?
3. What city is the biggest tourist destination in Europe?

Level 2

4. What famous event is held in Rio de Janeiro every year?
5. What did Mumbai, India, used to be called?
6. What is the oldest city in South Africa?
7. What is the biggest island in Japan?

Level 3

8. What percentage of Japan's population lives in its capital city?
9. What is a person who lives in Sydney, Australia, called?
10. Where is the biggest underground train network in the world?

FIND THE ANSWER:  Where in the world?

Cities are large settlements that are bigger or more populated than towns and villages. Most cities developed from small farming or hunting settlements, although others were planned from scratch. The world's most famous cities can be larger or richer than some countries—if New York City was a country, it would be the 16th richest in the world.

Tokyo 7 8 10
Tokyo is the capital city of Japan, "The Land of the Rising Sun." It is on the largest of Japan's four main islands, Honshu, and is home to around ten percent of the country's population. Tokyo has the biggest underground train network anywhere in the world.

New York City 1
New York City, "The Big Apple," is the most populated city and is the financial heart of the U.S., although Washington, D.C., is the capital.

Paris 3
Paris is the capital of France and is the biggest tourist destination in Europe. Its famous attractions include the Eiffel Tower, the *Mona Lisa*, and the Louvre museum.

EUROPE ASIA

NORTH AMERICA

AFRICA

AUSTRALASIA

SOUTH AMERICA

Rio de Janeiro 2 4
Rio de Janeiro is a large city in Brazil (Brasília is the capital). The city is famous for holding a huge carnival every year.

Cape Town 6
Cape Town is the oldest city in South Africa and gets its name from the Cape of Good Hope, the most southwesterly point of Africa.

Mumbai 5
Mumbai, in India, used to be called Bombay. The city has a population of more than 20 million people. It also has the biggest port in India.

Sydney 9
Sydney is most famous for the opera house in its harbor. People who live in Sydney are known as "Sydneysiders."

Answers 1) New York City **2)** Brazil **3)** Paris, France **4)** A carnival **5)** Bombay **6)** Cape Town **7)** Honshu **8)** Ten percent **9)** A Sydneysider **10)** Tokyo, Japan

QUIZ THREE
Science and inventions

QUESTIONS:
Exploring space

Level 1

1. The first living creature in space was a mouse. True or false?
2. Who was the first person on the Moon: Neil Armstrong, Nelly Armstrong, or Norman Armstrong?
3. ENVISION OUT can be rearranged to give the name of what group of republics?
4. What "S" is an object that orbits Earth?

Level 2

5. What "L" was the name of the first living creature in space?
6. What "S" was the first artificial satellite?
7. AN AIR RIG GUY can be rearranged to give the name of what astronaut, the first person to go into space?
8. In which year did people first walk on the Moon: 1959, 1969, or 1979?
9. In which year did a person first go into space: 1941, 1951, or 1961?
10. Who said, "That's one small step for man, one giant leap for mankind"?
11. VAN OR RULER can be rearranged to give the name of what vehicle used on the surface of the Moon?
12. For how long did the first person who went into space stay there: 89 minutes, 89 hours, or 89 days?

Level 3

13. Which was the last *Apollo* mission to land people on the Moon?
14. In what year did *Apollo 17* reach the Moon?
15. What are Soviet astronauts called?
16. What "V" was the first manned spacecraft?
17. What was launched on April 12, 1981?
18. Where is the Baikonur Cosmodrome: in Kazakhstan, Ukraine, or the Russian Federation?

Exploring space

Sputnik

It seems strange to think that 50 years ago no one had been into space. Today an International Space Station constantly circles Earth, manned by a crew of people from different countries. The history of space flight has happened within the lifetimes of many people alive today. It is an exciting story—and one that is far from being over.

Sputnik   3 4 6

Sputnik 1 was the world's first-ever human-made satellite (an object traveling around Earth). It was launched from Kazakhstan on October 4, 1957 by a group of republics called the Soviet Union.

Laika   1 5 18

The first living thing to enter space was Laika, a dog. Laika was launched in 1957 aboard the satellite *Sputnik 2* from the Baikonur Cosmodrome in Kazakhstan.

Laika the dog

Yuri Gagarin

Moon landing   2 8 10

In 1969 Neil Armstrong of the U.S. mission *Apollo 11* became the first person to walk on the Moon, with the famous words, "That's one small step for man, one giant leap for mankind."

rocket boosters

shuttle

USA

Person in space   7 9 12 16

On April 12, 1961, Yuri Gagarin became the first person ever to travel into space, aboard the spacecraft *Vostock 1*. A pilot from the Soviet Air Force, he traveled around Earth for 89 minutes.

space shuttle launch

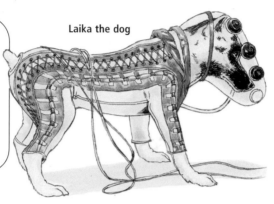

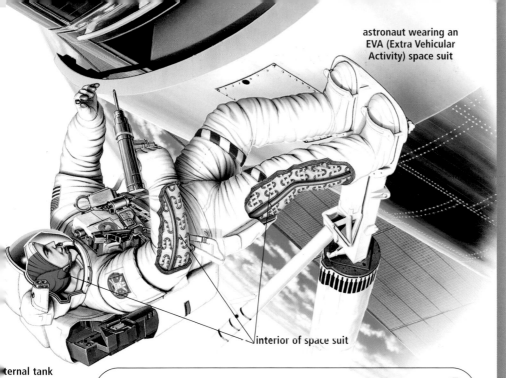

astronaut wearing an EVA (Extra Vehicular Activity) space suit

interior of space suit

ternal tank

Space suits 15

Space suits are designed to keep people alive in space. At first, they were worn by astronauts and cosmonauts (Soviet astronauts) inside their spacecraft. Today they are mostly used outside in space itself—for making repairs to a space shuttle, for example.

Moon missions 11 13 14

In total, Americans have made six successful missions to the Moon. The fourth, *Apollo 15*, carried a vehicle called a lunar rover to drive astronauts around on the surface. The last manned mission was *Apollo 17*, which landed on December 7, 1972. Since then, no one has visited the Moon.

Space shuttle 17

Early missions into space used huge, expensive rockets, which could only be used once. On January 5, 1972, the American government announced that it was going to develop a reusable spacecraft. The result was the space shuttle, which was first launched on April 12, 1981. Since then, there have been more than 100 launches.

QUESTIONS:
Solar system

Level 1

1. Which planet do people live on?
2. How many planets are in the solar system: seven, nine, or 11?
3. MY CURER can be rearranged to give the name of which planet?

Level 2

4. On the part of a planet facing away from the Sun, is it nighttime or daytime?
5. How many planets in our solar system have names that begin with the letter "M"?
6. Which planet is the farthest from the Sun?
7. A GANG SITS can be rearranged to give the name of what group of large planets?
8. What is the smallest planet in the solar system?
9. The Sun is a star. True or false?
10. Are there any planets in the solar system that are bigger than the Sun?
11. Did the planets form at around the same time as the Sun or long before?
12. Which "S" is a planet made mostly of hydrogen and helium?
13. How long does Earth take to circle the Sun: one day, one month, or one year?
14. What "O" is the path that planets take around the Sun?
15. Which takes longer to circle the Sun: Earth or Pluto?
16. How many planets in the solar system have oceans of water?

Level 3

17. What "N" is a swirling cloud of particles from which planets form?
18. Which is farther from the Sun: Uranus or Saturn?
19. Which is larger: Earth or Mars?

FIND THE ANSWER:  Solar system

The solar system is the group of planets, including Earth, that circle the Sun. Some of these planets are smaller than Earth, and others are many times larger. The solar system has existed for around 4.6 billion years, first appearing around 10.4 billion years after the "big bang" that began the universe.

Neptune

Uranus

Pluto

The planets   (2) (3) (5) (6) (18)
There are nine planets in the solar system. Mercury is the closest to the Sun, followed by Venus, Earth, Mars, Jupiter (the largest), Saturn, Uranus, Neptune, and Pluto (the farthest from the Sun).

Jupiter

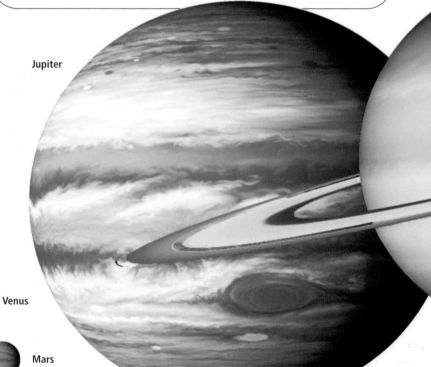

Venus

Mars

Earth

Mercury

Saturn

The Sun   (9) (10)
The Sun is a star, much bigger than any of the planets. It is 863,000 mi. (1,392,000km) wide and more than one million times bigger than Earth. For a star, it is fairly small.

Gas giants   (7) (12)
Jupiter, Saturn, Uranus, and Neptune are called the gas giants. Their small, rocky cores are surrounded by thick gases, mostly hydrogen and helium.

The smaller planets   (8) (19)
The smaller planets are Mercury, Venus, Earth, Mars, and Pluto. All of them have solid surfaces. Earth is the largest, and the smallest is Pluto.

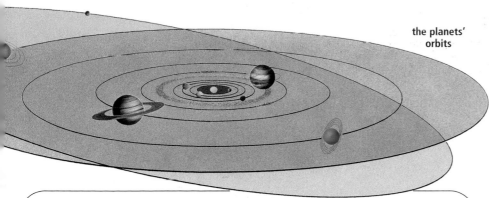

the planets' orbits

Orbits
13 14 15

All of the planets orbit the Sun (travel in a circle around it). The closer the planet is to the Sun, the shorter its orbit is. Earth's orbit takes exactly one year. Pluto takes more than 248 years to orbit.

nebula

gas and dust particles drawn together

Planets forming
11 17

The planets formed at around the same time as the Sun, from a nebula (a swirling cloud of gas and dust particles). Over time, the particles of the nebula slowly gathered together to form planets, drawn together by the force of gravity.

newly formed planet

Earth
1 4 16

People live on planet Earth, the only known planet to support life. It is the fifth largest in the solar system and the only one with oceans of water. As well as circling the Sun once each year, Earth spins around once every 24 hours. It is daytime on the part of Earth facing the Sun, and nighttime on the part facing away.

surface of Earth

QUESTIONS:
Volcanoes and earthquakes

Level 1
1. Is the surface of Earth made of solid or liquid rock?
2. What is another name for Earth's surface: the skin, crust, or coat?
3. RUIN POET can be rearranged to give what word for a volcano exploding?
4. A seismologist is a type of earthquake. True or false?

Level 2
5. What "R" is the scale used to measure the strength of earthquakes?
6. Which are thicker: continental plates or oceanic plates?
7. Are most earthquakes strong enough to destroy buildings?
8. How thick is Earth's mantle: 180 mi. (290km) or 1,800 mi. (2,900km)?
9. Do ridges form where plates move together or where they move apart?
10. Earthquakes are common where plates slide past one another. True or false?
11. Japan is situated where two plates meet. True or false?
12. What "L" is the molten rock released by a volcanic eruption?
13. What "F" is the force produced by plates sliding past each other?
14. CUBOID NUTS can be rearranged to give the name of what plate movement?
15. Volcanoes may occur where two plates are moving apart. True or false?

Level 3
16. What is the most common substance in Earth's core?
17. Which makes up a greater proportion of Earth: the crust or mantle?
18. On which plate do volcanoes occur when an oceanic plate and a continental plate meet?

FIND THE ANSWER:  Volcanoes and earthquakes

Earth's crust is in constant motion. Volcanoes and earthquakes arise as sections of crust ("plates") push together or pull apart. Volcanoes and earthquakes are more common in certain parts of the world. By monitoring ground vibrations (seismic activity), scientists can sometimes predict a massive earthquake or volcanic eruption and warn people.

volcano erupting

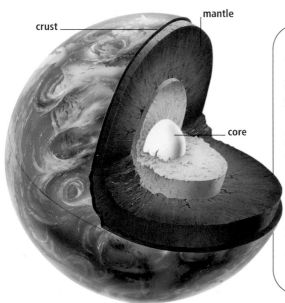

crust
mantle
core

Earth 1 2 8 16 17

The solid surface layer of Earth is known as the crust and ranges from 3–50 mi. (5–80km) in thickness. Beneath the crust is the mantle, which is 1,800 mi. (2,900km) thick and made up of molten rock. The center of Earth, the core, is mostly made of iron. It has a liquid outer core and a solid inner core and is around 8,100°F (4,500°C).

Volcanoes 3 12 18

Volcanoes form when molten rock is pushed up through the crust. When subduction occurs, the oceanic plate melts underground, creating a vast supply of molten rock. The rock is then released as lava in a volcanic eruption.

Moving apart 9 15

When plates move apart, ridges form. Often volcanoes occur there as molten rock moves up from the mantle to fill the gaps.

Subduction 6 14

When continental and oceanic plates move toward each other, the oceanic plate often slides underneath the thicker continental plate—this is called subduction.

plates moving apart

oceanic plate

plate melting

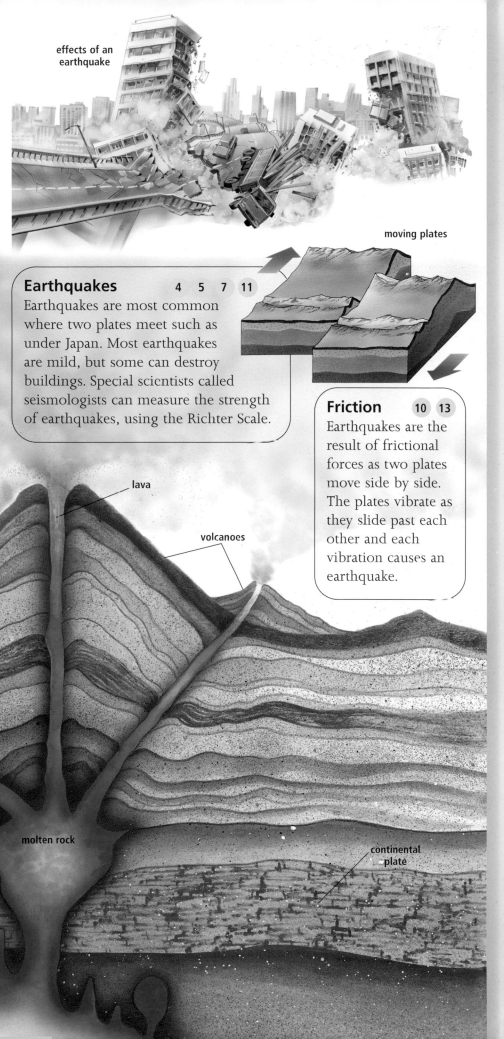

effects of an earthquake

moving plates

Earthquakes 4 5 7 11

Earthquakes are most common where two plates meet such as under Japan. Most earthquakes are mild, but some can destroy buildings. Special scientists called seismologists can measure the strength of earthquakes, using the Richter Scale.

lava

volcanoes

Friction 10 13

Earthquakes are the result of frictional forces as two plates move side by side. The plates vibrate as they slide past each other and each vibration causes an earthquake.

molten rock

continental plate

QUESTIONS:
Rocks and minerals

Level 1
1. Emeralds are purple. True or false?
2. What color are rubies?
3. Gold is a metal. True or false?
4. How many sides does a hexagon have: one, three, or six?

Level 2
5. TEARING can be rearranged to give the name of what igneous rock, often used for building?
6. Crystals form underground. True or false?
7. Do sedimentary rocks form on the bottoms of seas, lakes, and rivers or deep within Earth?
8. What word is used for rocks that form under great pressure or heat: metamorphic, mathematic, or metaphysical?
9. Is basalt an igneous or a sedimentary rock?
10. Gems are cut and polished to make gemstones. True or false?
11. What "C" is the substance from which diamonds are formed?
12. Which are the most valuable: diamonds, emeralds, or garnets?
13. HIS PAPER can be rearranged to give the name of what valuable gemstone?
14. A START can be rearranged to give what word for layers of rocks?

Level 3
15. In which country is the Giant's Causeway?
16. What "M" is molten rock, which cools to form igneous rock?
17. What is the name for a stone that has had its edges worn smooth by the action of water?
18. What "E" cannot be broken down into any simpler substance?

Rocks and minerals

Rocks are the building blocks of Earth's crust, and the substances of which they are composed are called minerals. The appearance and qualities of a rock are determined by the way it was formed. Humans use rocks and minerals to make everything from jewelry to houses.

basalt columns

Metamorphic rocks   8
The three main types of rocks are metamorphic, sedimentary, and igneous. Metamorphic rocks, such as marble, form underground, when existing rock is exposed to great pressure or heat.

erupting volcano

Igneous rocks   4 9 15 16
The Giant's Causeway in Northern Ireland is made up of hexagonal (six-sided) columns of basalt, an igneous rock. Like all igneous rocks, it formed from volcanic magma (melted rock), which erupted and then cooled down.

igneous rock

Sedimentary rocks   7 14
These rocks form from sediments, such as sand and mud, at the bottoms of seas, lakes, and rivers, building up over long periods of time. Gradually, the weight of the water compresses them into rocks. Sedimentary rocks form in strata (layers).

Stones   5 17
A stone is a small piece of rock, and a pebble is a stone that has had its edges smoothed over time by the action of water. The hardest stones are those from igneous rocks such as granite or from metamorphic rocks such as slate.

granite

pumice

obsidian

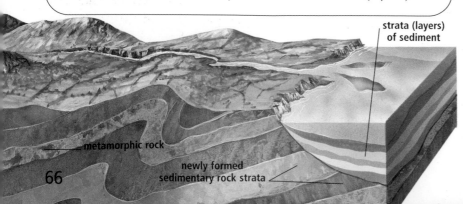

strata (layers) of sediment

metamorphic rock

newly formed sedimentary rock strata

serpentinite

amethyst

Minerals ③ ⑱
There are two types of minerals: those with crystalline structures and naturally occurring metals such as gold. These metals are elements—they cannot be broken down into any simpler substance.

Crystals ⑥
Crystalline minerals form in underground rocks under great heat or pressure. Crystals have flat sides and can be extremely beautiful.

 realgar
 azurite
 quartz
 diamond

 galena
 malachite
pyrite
fluorite

Gemstones ⑩
Some crystalline minerals are known as gemstones. They are precious or semiprecious stones that can be cut and polished to make gems, which are used in jewelry. The rarest ones are considered the most valuable.

1. gemstone in rock

2. rough gemstone

3. glittering jewel

 turquoise

 garnet

 amethyst

 topaz

aquamarine

 opal

diamond

 sapphire

emerald

 peridot

ruby

pearl

Types of gemstones ① ② ⑪ ⑫ ⑬
The most famous and expensive gemstone is the diamond. It is unusual because it is a crystal made from a single element—carbon. Other very rare and precious gemstones include emeralds, which are green, rubies, which are red, and sapphires, which are blue.

QUESTIONS: Weather

Level 1
1. Does weather happen in the atmosphere or under the sea?
2. Are clouds made of cotton balls or water vapor?
3. What "O" is the gas we must breathe in order to stay alive?
4. What "L" is the word for an electrical charge released from a storm cloud?
5. A weather balloon is a type of cloud. True or false?

Level 2
6. Where does the majority of the water vapor in clouds originally come from?
7. Does a weather vane measure wind speed or wind direction?
8. Which is usually associated with good weather: high pressure or low pressure?
9. What "R" is sometimes formed as sunlight passes through raindrops?
10. Do rainbows appear when it rains or when there is no rain?
11. Do raindrops become bigger or smaller as they fall through a cloud?
12. What "H" is a word for frozen raindrops?
13. Do clouds become cooler or hotter as they rise?
14. REACH RUIN can be rearranged to give the name of what powerful storm?
15. RING TONE can be rearranged to give the name of which very common gas?

Level 3
16. What is a scientist who studies the weather called?
17. How many colors are there in a rainbow?
18. What "S" do weather forecasters use to watch storms building up in the atmosphere?

FIND THE ANSWER:

Weather

The weather affects all of us. It makes us decide what clothes to put on in the morning and whether we should go outside or stay inside. In some places, the weather can be very hard to predict. As we learn more about our planet, however, we are gradually getting better at figuring out what the weather is going to do next.

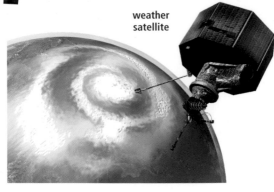

weather satellite

Storm cloud 4 13
As clouds rise, they cool, and the water vapor turns into droplets. The droplets bump into each other, causing an electric charge to build up. If the charge becomes large enough, it is released as lightning.

Watching weather 14 18
Today satellites watch the weather from up above. They help weather forecasters see storms building up in the atmosphere. Large storms and hurricanes appear as huge swirls of clouds.

Atmosphere 1 3 15
Weather occurs in the atmosphere—the layer of gases surrounding Earth. The most common gas is nitrogen, followed by oxygen, which we breathe in order to stay alive.

storm cloud

Clouds 2 6
Clouds are collections of water vapor. The vapor forms as the Sun's energy evaporates liquid water, mostly from the surface of the sea.

rain

Weather research

5 16

Scientists who study the weather are known as meteorologists. Weather balloons are just one of the tools that meteorologists use to gather information about the weather. The balloons carry devices that measure weather conditions far above the ground.

anemometer

weather vane

thermometer

barometer

Measuring the weather

7 8

There are many devices for measuring the weather. Thermometers measure temperature, while barometers measure air pressure— high pressure means good weather, and low pressure signals storms. An anemometer measures wind speed, while a weather vane shows wind direction.

weather balloon

Rain

11 12

Rain falls when the droplets in clouds become too large and heavy to remain up in the air. As they fall through the air, they hit other droplets and grow bigger. Sometimes they freeze and fall as hail or snow.

Rainbows

9 10 17

Rainbows form when it rains on sunny days. They are the result of the light from the Sun being split into its seven colors as it passes through raindrops.

rain cloud

rainbow

QUESTIONS:
Bones and muscles

Level 1

1. BELOW can be rearranged to give the name of what joint in the middle of the arm?
2. Are there muscles in the human leg?
3. What "S" is the name for all the bones in the body put together?

Level 2

4. Do people have joints in their fingers?
5. Muscles contain millions of cells called fibers. True or false?
6. What "B" is a muscle in the arm that helps raise the forearm?
7. Which bones form a cage that protect the internal organs?
8. What "C" is the correct name for the gristle in human bodies?
9. Which bone links the legs to the backbone?
10. The patella is another name for which bone?
11. The muscles in the heart work automatically. True or false?
12. When a person raises their forearm, do their triceps contract or relax?
13. How many bones are there in an adult's skull: two, 12, or 22?
14. Do people have more muscles or more bones in their bodies?
15. Is the shoulder joint a hinge joint or a ball-and-socket joint?
16. What is the largest bone in the human body?
17. What is the name of the eight bones that, together, encase the brain?

Level 3

18. The mandible is another name for which part of the body?
19. In which part of the body is the smallest bone?
20. How many bones are there in the human skeleton?

Bones and muscles

The human body is an incredible natural machine. It can perform a huge variety of different movements and operations—many more than any robot or other human-made machine. Like those of other mammals, the human body is based on a complex system of muscles attached to a strong but flexible bony skeleton.

knee

elbow

shoulder

hip

shinbone (tibia)

fibula

Joints 1 4 15
Joints are the areas in the skeleton where different bones meet. They are what make the skeleton flexible and allow limbs and other parts of the body to move. The shoulder and the hip joints are called ball-and-socket joints. The elbow, knee, and finger joints are known as hinge joints.

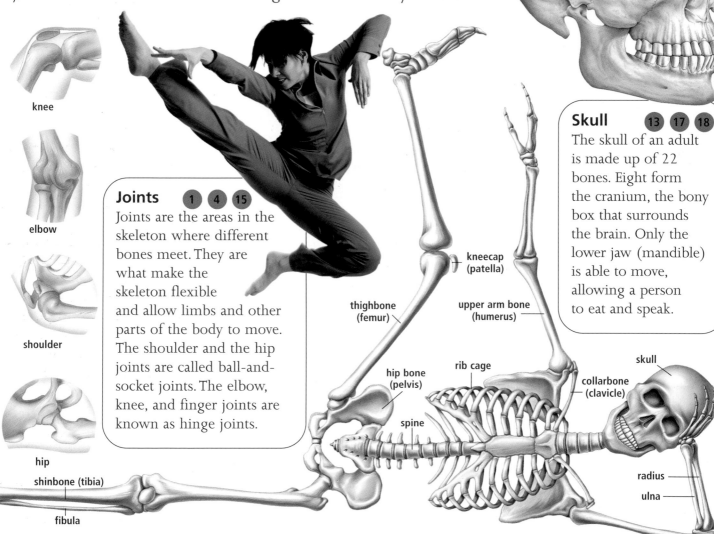

kneecap (patella)

thighbone (femur)

upper arm bone (humerus)

hip bone (pelvis)

rib cage

spine

collarbone (clavicle)

skull

radius

ulna

Skull 13 17 18
The skull of an adult is made up of 22 bones. Eight form the cranium, the bony box that surrounds the brain. Only the lower jaw (mandible) is able to move, allowing a person to eat and speak.

Knees 8 10
These joints separate the upper and lower halves of the legs. The ends of the bones are covered with a layer of cartilage (gristle) to stop them from rubbing together. The patella (kneecap) is a small bone that protects the knee from injuries.

Skeleton 3 7 9 14 16 19 20
The human skeleton is made up of 206 bones. The largest are the two thighbones (femurs), linked to the backbone by the pelvis. The smallest are the stirrup bones, which help transmit sounds from the eardrums to the brain. The ribs mostly remain in the same position, forming a protective cage around the organs.

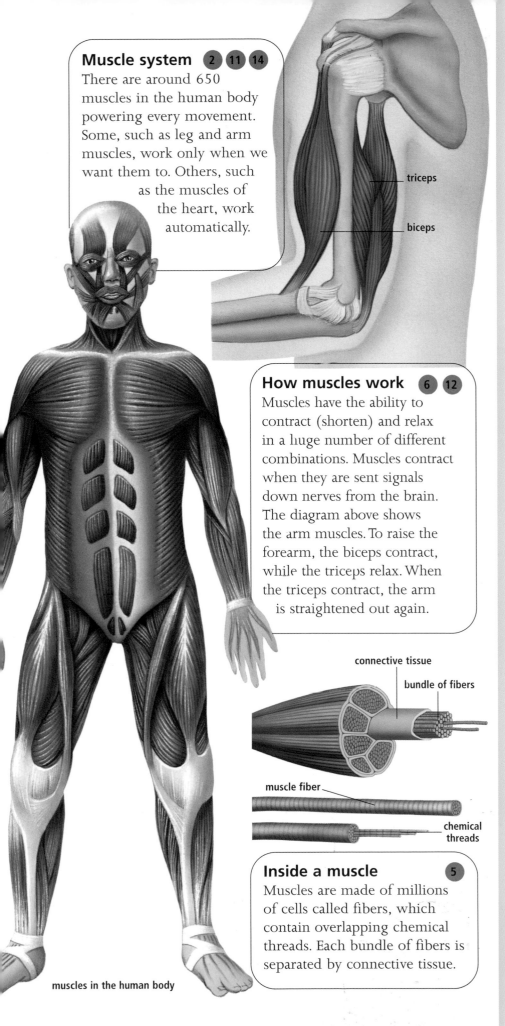

Muscle system ②⑪⑭

There are around 650 muscles in the human body powering every movement. Some, such as leg and arm muscles, work only when we want them to. Others, such as the muscles of the heart, work automatically.

triceps

biceps

How muscles work ⑥⑫

Muscles have the ability to contract (shorten) and relax in a huge number of different combinations. Muscles contract when they are sent signals down nerves from the brain. The diagram above shows the arm muscles. To raise the forearm, the biceps contract, while the triceps relax. When the triceps contract, the arm is straightened out again.

connective tissue

bundle of fibers

muscle fiber

chemical threads

Inside a muscle ⑤

Muscles are made of millions of cells called fibers, which contain overlapping chemical threads. Each bundle of fibers is separated by connective tissue.

muscles in the human body

QUESTIONS:
Medicine

Level 1
1. What "D" is the person people visit when they are feeling sick?
2. What vehicles take people to the hospital: ambulances, fire engines, or tractors?
3. Are ambulances part of the emergency services?
4. Do nurses work in hospitals or stores?

Level 2
5. Broken bones heal themselves. True or false?
6. What "S" is used to listen to a person's heartbeat?
7. What does a thermometer measure?
8. Is intensive care given to people who are very sick or to people who are better, just before they leave the hospital?
9. What "S" is the word for a person who carries out operations?
10. What "T" means to replace a damaged body part with a new, healthy one?
11. Would you wear a cast if you had the flu or if you had a broken leg?
12. A SCARED IMP can be rearranged to give the name of what people who care for patients on the way to the hospital?
13. A symptom is a type of medicine. True or false?
14. What "S" is a large machine that looks inside people's bodies?

Level 3
15. What "D" means "to figure out what is wrong with a patient"?
16. What type of injury can be treated by traction?
17. What is used to transfer nutrients straight into a person's bloodstream?
18. What "M" is a type of wave that scanners use to look inside a body?

FIND THE ANSWER: Medicine

The word "medicine" has two meanings. When someone is sick, a doctor may give them medicine to make them feel better. But medicine is also a branch of science that studies diseases and injuries. Doctors, nurses, and surgeons work in the field of medicine, and so do the pharmacists and researchers who develop new drugs and cures.

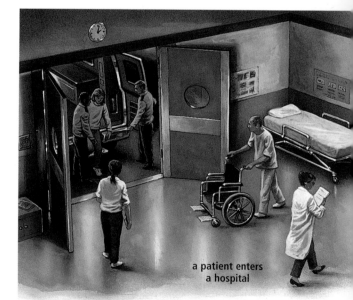
the scene of an accident

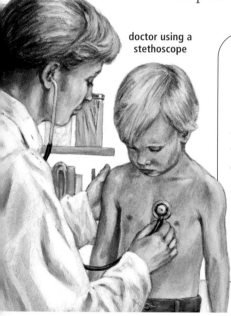
doctor using a stethoscope

Doctors 1 6 7 13 15

A doctor is the first person you go to see if you are feeling sick. Doctors look for symptoms (signs) of different illnesses and diagnose (figure out) what is wrong. This doctor is using a stethoscope to listen to the boy's heartbeat. Doctors also use thermometers to measure body temperature.

Emergency services 2 3 12

Ambulances are vehicles that carry sick or injured people to the hospital. They are part of the emergency services. Most ambulances have paramedics on board, who are trained to treat patients as they are taken to the hospital.

Treating broken bones 5 11 16

Broken bones heal themselves, but to make sure that they join back together in the right way, doctors wrap the affected limbs in rigid casts. Sometimes they use traction (shown below)—a system of pulleys and wires that keep the bones in the correct position.

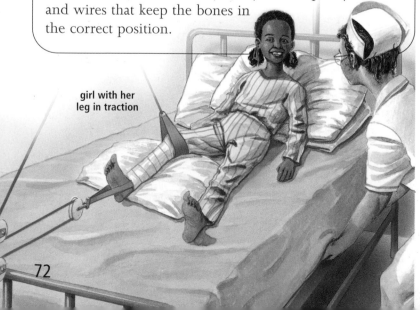
girl with her leg in traction

a patient enters a hospital

Hospitals 4

Hospitals are where sick and injured people go to be treated and get better. They are also the places where many doctors and most surgeons and nurses work. Most large towns and cities have at least one hospital.

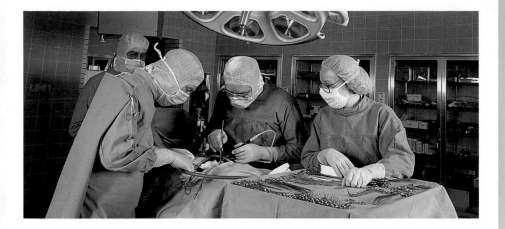

Operations 9 10

Surgeons carry out operations to make people better. Some operations involve removing diseased parts of the body. Others, known as transplants, involve taking out an old or damaged part and replacing it with a healthy, new one.

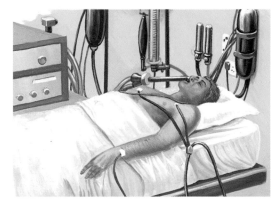

Intensive care 8 17

Very sick people need intensive care. They are watched closely by nurses and are assisted by machines. They may have an IV, which feeds nutrients through a tube straight into the blood.

Body scans 14 18

Scanners are machines that can look inside the body. They do this using X-rays or magnetic waves, which pass through the body and are picked up by sensors. The pictures generated may reveal signs of injury or disease that would otherwise be invisible.

a patient has a CAT (computerized axial tomography) scan

QUESTIONS:
Trains

Level 1

1. Which came first: steam engines or electric trains?
2. Do all trains carry passengers?
3. Is diesel a type of fuel or a type of food?
4. Who built the train that ran on the first-ever steam railroad: Richard Trevithick, Richard Gere, or Richard the Lionheart?
5. What "C" was burned in steam engines?

Level 2

6. Was the Wild West in Europe or in the United States?
7. Is steam created by heating water or by heating gasoline?
8. Which country has bullet trains and super expresses?
9. What "R" was a famous steam engine built by George Stephenson?
10. Which country has TGVs?
11. Are there any trains that can go faster than 125 mph (200km/h)?
12. What "C" on Wild West trains was used for moving cattle off the line?
13. Were steam trains cleaner or dirtier than modern trains?

Level 3

14. In which country was the world's first-ever steam railroad?
15. In which century was the first railroad to cross North America built?
16. What "F" is the word used for the goods carried by some trains?
17. How long was the world's longest-ever train: 3 mi. (5km), 4 mi. (6km), or 5 mi. (7km)?
18. What "P" were exploring settlers who traveled into the Wild West by train?

FIND THE ANSWER: Trains

Trains are great for getting around. They travel along networks of railroad tracks. As well as being fast, they are comfortable and usually quiet. Trains have been around for 200 years, longer than there have been cars on the roads. They can carry many people while using a fairly small amount of fuel, which is good for the environment.

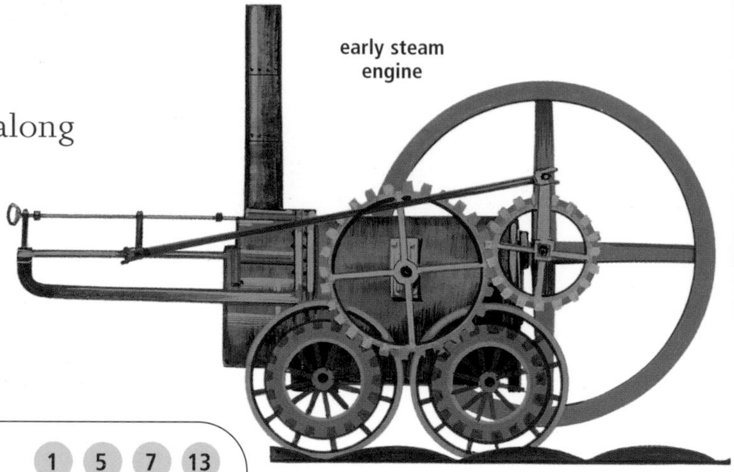

early steam engine

George Stephenson's *Rocket*

Steam 1 5 7 13
The first trains were powered by steam. This was created by burning coal in order to heat tanks of water to very high temperatures. Because they were burning coal, steam trains were much dirtier than modern electric trains.

Rails 4 9 14
Richard Trevithick was the first person to put a steam engine on rails, and in doing so he invented the railroad. His first engine set off in south Wales in February 1804—25 years before George Stephenson's famous engine, the *Rocket*.

bullet train

JR500 WEST JAPAN

Wild West trains ⑥ ⑫ ⑮ ⑱

Trains helped open up the Wild West of the U.S. to pioneers (exploring settlers). The first railroad to go right across North America was finished in 1869. The trains had large chimneys and "cowcatchers" to sweep cattle off the line.

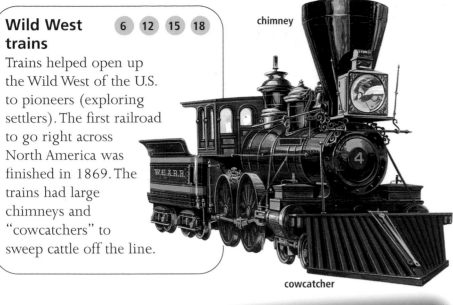

chimney

cowcatcher

freight train

Bullet trains ⑧ ⑩ ⑪

Japan has an extremely good rail network. The fastest trains are known as bullet trains or super expresses and regularly run at more than 185 mph (300km/h). France also has very fast trains, known as TGVs.

Freight ② ③ ⑯ ⑰

Not all trains carry passengers. Freight trains are used to transport goods. The world's longest train carried coal across the U.S. It was around 4 mi. (6km) long and was pulled by three huge diesel-fueled engines.

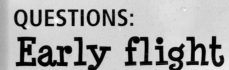

QUESTIONS:
Early flight

Level 1

1. GIRDLE can be rearranged to give the name of what type of unpowered aircraft?
2. The first manned flight was in a hot-air balloon. True or false?
3. Is a dirigible a steerable airship or an Australian musical instrument?

Level 2

4. What "H" is a type of aircraft with rotating blades?
5. Which body of water was Louis Blériot the first to fly across in 1909: the English Channel or the Atlantic Ocean?
6. In which century did Otto Lilienthal make the first controlled glider flights: the ninth or 19th century?
7. How many wings does a monoplane have: two or four?
8. Which "G" is a country, home to Otto Lilienthal?
9. Jean-François Pilâtre was the first man to fly. True or false?
10. Was the first powered airplane flight in Europe or the United States?
11. Which great 16th-century Italian artist and thinker designed a glider that was never built?
12. Which "M" were brothers who built the first manned aircraft?

Level 3

13. What was the last name of Wilbur and Orville, who designed the first-ever heavier-than-air powered aircraft?
14. What was the Wright brothers' aircraft called?
15. What did the first heavier-than-air powered aircraft use as fuel?
16. In which century did the first-ever manned aircraft take off: the 16th, 17th, or 18th century?
17. Who made the first-ever powered flight?
18. What was the nationality of the person who made the first-ever powered flight?

Early flight

Today many people take flight for granted. Every day thousands of airplanes carry passengers all over the world. Yet it was only around 100 years ago that the first gasoline-driven aircraft took to the skies. The very first flights were made in hot-air balloons, airships, and unpowered winged gliders.

Montgolfier　2　9　12　16

The first-ever manned aircraft was a hot-air balloon built by the French Montgolfier brothers. On October 15, 1783, it lifted Jean-François Pilâtre 82 ft. (25m) above the city of Paris, France. It was anchored with rope to stop it from floating away.

the Montgolfier hot-air balloon

da Vinci's glider

Rope

Early glider　4　11

People dreamed of flying long before they achieved it. The glider shown above was designed by Italian thinker and artist Leonardo da Vinci around the year 1500. He also designed a type of helicopter with rotating blades, but neither of his flying machines was actually built.

Powered flight　3　10　14　17　18

The first heavier-than-air powered aircraft, the *Wright Flyer*, took off on December 17, 1903 in the U.S. The first powered flight had already been made 50 years earlier by the Frenchman Henri Giffard in a steam-powered dirigible (steerable airship).

the Wright Flyer

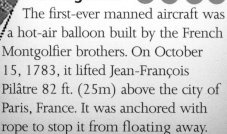

Lilienthal　① ⑥ ⑧
German engineer Otto Lilienthal built gliders (unpowered winged aircraft). He made the first controlled glider flights in 1861. Other people had flown gliders but had not been able to control them.

Lilienthal's glider

monoplane

Blériot　⑤ ⑦
In 1909 Frenchman Louis Blériot became the first person to fly an airplane across the English Channel. Blériot also designed and built some of the world's first successful monoplanes (airplanes with only two wings, instead of four or six).

The Wright brothers　⑬ ⑮
Wilbur and Orville Wright designed and built the first heavier-than-air powered aircraft. It had a special lightweight gasoline engine. The brothers went on to build aircraft for other people.

QUESTIONS:
Sailing

Level 1
1. Sailboats use the wind to push them along. True or false?
2. Are boats kept moored in a marina, a merino, or a mariner?
3. What type of jackets do people wear to keep them afloat in the water?
4. Do any sailboats have engines?
5. What suit keeps windsurfers warm?
6. A rudder is used to help steer a boat. True or false?
7. What "Y" is a large sailboat used for pleasure?

Level 2
8. Which were invented first: square sails or triangular sails?
9. What "P" is the left-hand side of a boat and a place where ships dock?
10. What is the word for the rear of a boat?
11. BROAD ARTS can be rearranged to give what word for the right-hand side of a boat?
12. Boats with square sails can only go in the same direction as the wind. True or false?
13. How many hulls do trimarans have?
14. What is a boat with two hulls called?
15. What are small, open boats without cabins called?
16. What "W" are people who sail standing up on a board?

Level 3
17. What part of a boat helps keep it from tipping over?
18. Which Mediterranean island was home to the seafaring Minoans?
19. When did ancient sailing ships use their oars?

FIND THE ANSWER: Sailing

Before the 1800s, most of the world's boats and ships had sails. Sailing ships carried the explorers to America and Australia and the Europeans who later settled on those continents. Today most people who sail do so for pleasure or sports, although in some parts of the world boats with sails are still used to transport goods.

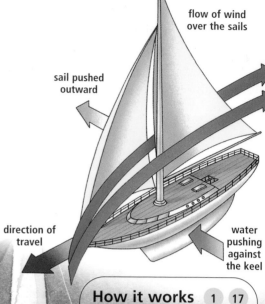

flow of wind over the sails

sail pushed outward

direction of travel

water pushing against the keel

How it works 1 17

The force of the wind pushes against the sails to move a boat through the water. Modern sailboats can travel in any direction except directly into the wind. Changing direction is called tacking. A keel underneath the boat prevents it from tipping over if the wind is too strong.

spinnaker

cabin

The first sailing ships 8 12 18 19

Built around 2500 B.C. by the Minoans of Crete and the ancient Greeks, the first sailboats had square sails, which meant that they could only sail in the same direction as the wind. They used oars to go forward against the wind. When triangular sails appeared around 1200 B.C., people could move them to sail in any direction.

Sailing for pleasure 2 4 7

Most people who own sailboats use them for fun and keep them docked in harbors or marinas. Larger sailboats are known as yachts. Some sailboats also have engines for sailing when there is no wind.

Dinghies ③ ⑥ ⑮
A dinghy is a small, open boat without a cabin. Most sailing dinghies carry one or two people. People who sail dinghies usually wear life jackets in case they fall overboard. Like most boats, dinghies have a rudder at the stern to help with steering.

life jacket

rudder

Catamarans ⑬ ⑭
A catamaran is a boat with two hulls. These people sailing a catamaran use their weight to stop it from tipping over by leaning out on the far side. Boats with three hulls are called trimarans.

hull

Bowsprits ⑨ ⑩ ⑪
The long pole that sticks out from the front of this boat is called the bowsprit. The bow is the front of a boat. The rear is known as the stern, the left side is the port, and the right side is called the starboard.

bowsprit

Windsurfing ⑤ ⑯
Windsurfers stand on a surfboard and hold the sail, moving it to catch the wind. They wear wet suits to keep them warm when they fall off, which they often do.

QUESTIONS:
Submarines

Level 1
1. Does the word "submarine" literally mean "under the sea" or "above the mountains"?
2. Is a torpedo a type of weapon or a running shoe?
3. What "D" is the word for people who explore underwater?
4. LATIN CAT can be rearranged to give the name of which ocean?

Level 2
5. Which country's submarines were known as U-boats?
6. Are there any submarines that are driven by nuclear power?
7. What is the name for the spinning objects that push submarines through the water?
8. Can submarines attack boats that are on the surface?
9. Are research submarines called submersibles or submissives?
10. What "D" is a type of fuel commonly used in submarines?
11. What is the name for the tanks that fill with seawater when a submarine descends?
12. A bathyscaphe is a type of radar system. True or false?
13. What do the letters ROV stand for?
14. SPICE ROPE can be rearranged to give the name of what device used by submarine crews to see above the water?

Level 3
15. Where is the Mariana Trench, the deepest point on Earth?
16. What was the name of the bathyscaphe that first carried people to the bottom of the Mariana Trench?
17. What was the name of the manned submersible that first explored the wreck of the *Titanic*?
18. Which ocean liner was torpedoed and sunk by a German U-boat on May 7, 1915?

Submarines

Submarines are used to explore the underwater world. They are also used by the navies of some countries for defense in times of war. Although people long dreamed of voyaging under the sea, submarines have been around for less than 400 years. Today's submarines are a far cry from the earliest designs, most of which were made of wood and were powered by the people who rode in them.

Power   6 7 10

Modern submarines are driven by propellers, like most ships. These propellers are turned by huge engines. Some submarines have diesel engines, while others are driven by nuclear power.

Warfare   5 8 18

During the world wars, the German navy made great use of their submarines, which were called U-boats. They used them to fire torpedoes at enemy warships, such as the *RMS Lusitania*, which was sunk on May 7, 1915.

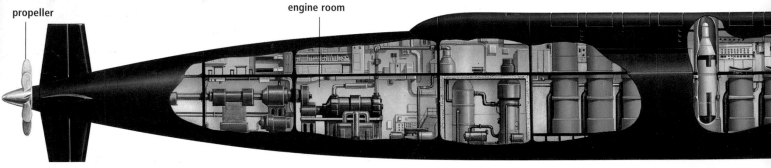

propeller

engine room

Diving and resurfacing   1 11

Submarine literally means "under the water." When a submarine dives, special tanks (ballast tanks) fill up with seawater. To resurface, compressed air is pumped into the tanks. This forces water out, making the submarine lighter.

diving— seawater in

up—air in, water out

Subsuits   3

Divers sometimes use subsuits like one-person submarines for exploration in deep water. These have arms with pincers that the diver can operate, allowing him or her to pick up things and manipulate objects deep beneath the sea.

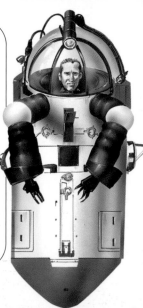

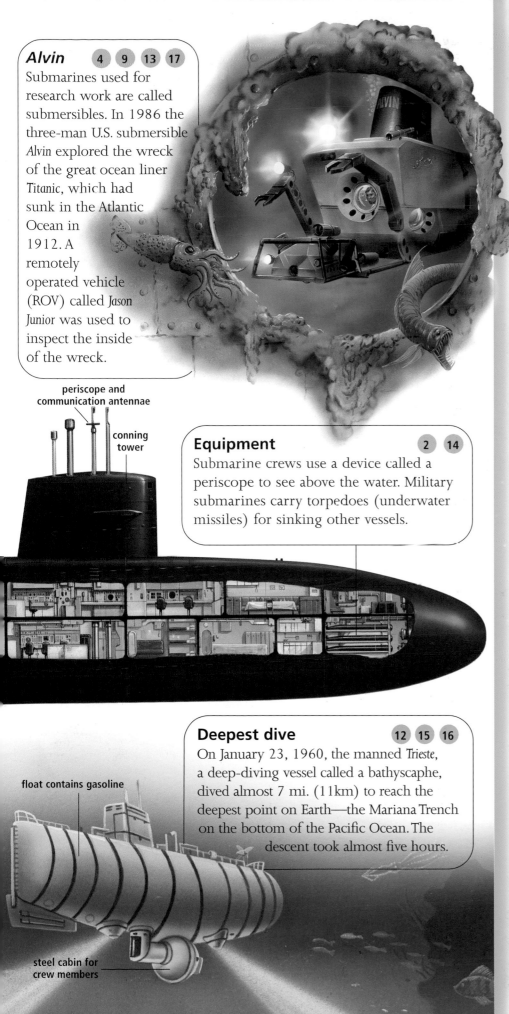

Alvin (4) (9) (13) (17)
Submarines used for research work are called submersibles. In 1986 the three-man U.S. submersible *Alvin* explored the wreck of the great ocean liner *Titanic*, which had sunk in the Atlantic Ocean in 1912. A remotely operated vehicle (ROV) called *Jason Junior* was used to inspect the inside of the wreck.

periscope and communication antennae

conning tower

Equipment (2) (14)
Submarine crews use a device called a periscope to see above the water. Military submarines carry torpedoes (underwater missiles) for sinking other vessels.

float contains gasoline

Deepest dive (12) (15) (16)
On January 23, 1960, the manned *Trieste*, a deep-diving vessel called a bathyscaphe, dived almost 7 mi. (11km) to reach the deepest point on Earth—the Mariana Trench on the bottom of the Pacific Ocean. The descent took almost five hours.

steel cabin for crew members

QUESTIONS:
Household inventions

Level 1
1. Would you put bread in a toaster or a dishwasher?
2. What "K" is used for heating water?
3. Which was invented first, the electric washing machine or the food processor?

Level 2
4. Which invention is usually credited to John Logie Baird?
5. SHARED WISH can be rearranged to give the name of what household appliance?
6. Did the automatic cutout on an electric kettle appear in 1890, 1930, or 1989?
7. Which was invented first: the electric washing machine or the dishwasher?
8. Which household object is usually associated with Thomas Edison?
9. People only started to use zippers in the 1940s. True or false?
10. Which handy implement was invented by Laszlo Biro?
11. The aerofoam extinguisher is used on what type of fires?
12. SCOOPS RED ROOF can be rearranged to give the name of what kitchen appliance?
13. In which decade of the 20th century did microwave ovens first go on sale?

Level 3
14. In what year was the first television picture transmitted?
15. James Murray Spangler invented the first portable what?
16. What did Alexandre Godefoy invent?
17. Which kitchen appliance was developed from an earlier invention called the magnetron?
18. Who invented the sewing machine?

Household inventions

Most homes are full of human-made objects designed to make people's lives easier or get jobs done faster. Technological advances in the 1900s brought dramatic changes, with the introduction of labor-saving appliances such as the washing machine, dishwasher, and vacuum cleaner.

The kettle 2 6

The electric kettle was invented by Arthur Leslie Large in 1922. A safety device called an automatic cutout appeared in 1930, to prevent electric shocks.

kettle

Entertainment 4 8 14 16

Thomas Edison made the first lightbulb for sale in 1879. The first television picture was transmitted in 1925 by engineer John Logie Baird. The electric hair dryer was invented in the 1920s by Alexandre Godefoy.

Microwave 13 17

The first microwave ovens went on sale in 1967. They were developed from an earlier invention called the magnetron.

Cook and clean 1 5 7 12

The electric washing machine was invented in 1908, the electric dishwasher in 1913, and the electric toaster in 1909. The food processor was invented later, in 1971.

telephone

food processor

microwave

radio

toaster

refrigerator

washing machine

oven

dishwasher

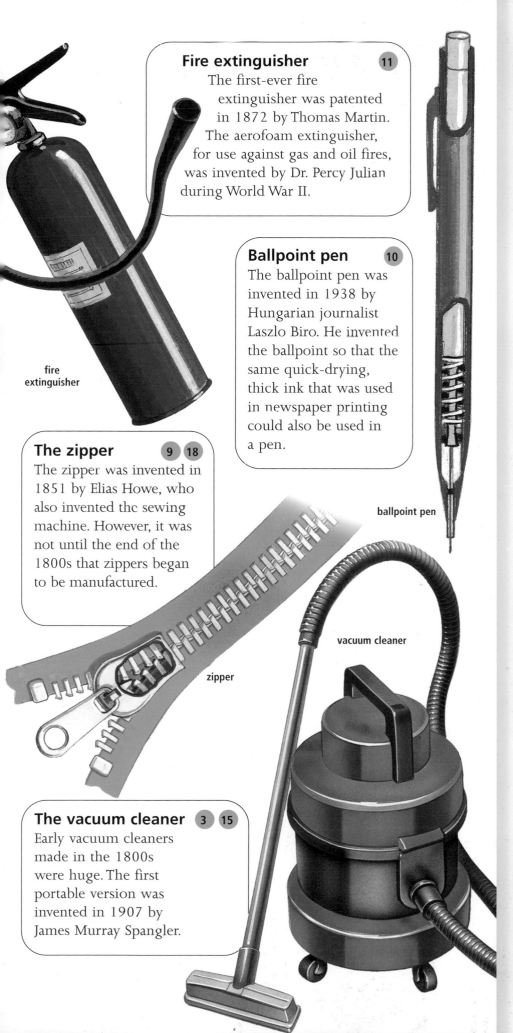

Fire extinguisher (11)

The first-ever fire extinguisher was patented in 1872 by Thomas Martin. The aerofoam extinguisher, for use against gas and oil fires, was invented by Dr. Percy Julian during World War II.

fire extinguisher

Ballpoint pen (10)

The ballpoint pen was invented in 1938 by Hungarian journalist Laszlo Biro. He invented the ballpoint so that the same quick-drying, thick ink that was used in newspaper printing could also be used in a pen.

ballpoint pen

The zipper (9) (18)

The zipper was invented in 1851 by Elias Howe, who also invented the sewing machine. However, it was not until the end of the 1800s that zippers began to be manufactured.

zipper

vacuum cleaner

The vacuum cleaner (3) (15)

Early vacuum cleaners made in the 1800s were huge. The first portable version was invented in 1907 by James Murray Spangler.

QUESTIONS:
Robots

Level 1

1. Are there any robots that work in factories?
2. Do robots ever get tired?
3. Are there any robots that can work underwater?
4. ODD SIR can be rearranged to give what name for robots such as R2-D2?
5. Robots can only do one thing at a time. True or false?

Level 2

6. Are there any robots that can play the piano?
7. Which series of movies starred the robot C-3PO?
8. What "C" is programmed with the information that is needed to make robots operate?
9. LEWDING can be rearranged to give the name of what task performed by robots?
10. Which have traveled farthest from Earth: robots or humans?
11. Solar panels are used to capture energy from which source?
12. Can robots perform sign language?
13. Which planet is currently being explored by robots?
14. What "M" is the word for doing more than one job at a time?
15. Can robots be programmed to detonate bombs?

Level 3

16. The word "robot" comes from which language?
17. Which country developed the WABOT-2 robot?
18. In what year was the animated movie *Robots* released?

Robots

Robots are machines that can perform some of the physical tasks that would normally be carried out by humans. Many robots are now used in factories, particularly where large objects, such as cars, are made. They are also used to explore where people cannot travel such as the seabed and the surfaces of other planets.

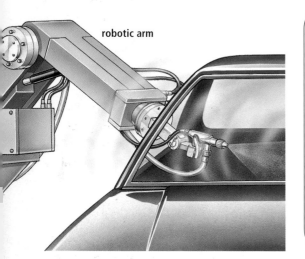

robotic arm

Industry 1 2 8 9
Many factories today use robots for heavy, repetitive, or difficult jobs. Unlike people, robots do not become tired or bored. Industrial robots are directed by computers to carry out particular tasks such as spraying car bodywork or welding pieces together.

Multitasking 5 14
Some robots can carry out more than one job at once. They are known as multitasking robots. Each robot arm does a different job or a similar job in a different direction.

Humanlike robots 6 17
The Japanese robot WABOT-2 can play the piano much faster than a human can. It can either read new music or choose a song that it has played before and stored in its memory. WABOT-2 can also play gently or furiously. Other robots can perform sign language, and some can behave like pets.

UPHAUT 2 explored a narrow shaft in the Great Pyramid of Giza in 1993

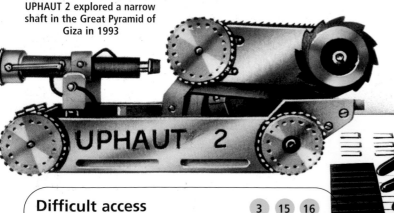

UPHAUT 2

Difficult access 3 15 16
The word "robot" comes from the Czech word *robota*, meaning "forced labor." Robots are very useful for doing dangerous jobs. Some are used to defuse or safely detonate bombs. Others can work deep underwater to explore shipwrecks or dangerous areas of the seabed.

Mars robots 10 11 13

Robots have traveled farther than any human being. Since January 2004, robots known as the Mars rovers have been exploring the surface of Mars. The robots, which carry cameras, are powered by solar panels, which capture energy from the Sun.

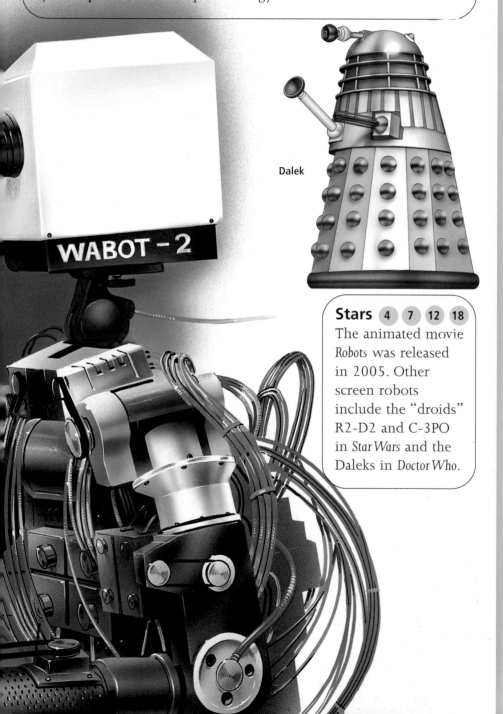

WABOT-2

Dalek

Stars 4 7 12 18

The animated movie *Robots* was released in 2005. Other screen robots include the "droids" R2-D2 and C-3PO in *Star Wars* and the Daleks in *Doctor Who*.

Level 1

1. What "I" is the network that links computers all over the world?
2. Does "PC" stand for perfect computer or personal computer?
3. What is a computer that is small enough to fit in the hand called: a handbag, a handheld, or a handshake?
4. What "M" is both a small, furry animal and an object that attaches to a computer?
5. What is stored in MP3 files?

Level 2

6. Where were computer games played before people had home computers?
7. Can people play computer games while they are on the move?
8. What type of computer is the word "Mac" short for?
9. Do most handheld game machines take cartridges or disks?
10. Is the information in a computer held in the hard drive, printer, or mouse?
11. What "B" is the computer equipment used to put information onto a CD?
12. Is a computer keyboard a peripheral or a profiterole?
13. What "V" is put in front of the word "reality" to describe lifelike situations produced by computers?
14. What "H" do you wear when playing a virtual-reality game?
15. TOP PAL can be rearranged to give what name for a portable computer?

Level 3

16. Which would you use to store data: a CD-RAM, a CD-REM, or a CD-ROM?
17. What connects a home computer to the Internet?
18. What type of files would you put onto an iPod?

Computers and video games

In the past 20 or 30 years, computers have completely changed the way that people work. They have also changed the way that we play, bringing a new world of entertainment into our homes. There are now video game consoles that plug into televisions, while small, portable machines (handhelds) allow us to play games anywhere.

The Internet · 1 · 17
The Internet is the network of telephone lines and servers that link home computers around the world together. The Internet allows people to exchange information quickly and freely.

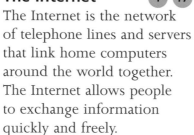

girl using laptop computer

Digital accessories · 5 · 18
All types of equipment can be plugged into computers. Pictures from digital cameras can be copied onto a computer's hard drive. Music can also be stored on a computer and can be passed to and from MP3 players such as the iPod.

Home computers · 2 · 8 · 15
Many people have PCs (personal computers). Others have Macs, or Macintoshes, like the one shown below. Smaller, portable computers are called laptops.

Hard drive · 10
The hard drive holds all the information that a computer needs to be able to work. It is the most important part of the machine.

hard drive

CD drive

Macintosh computer

iPod MP3 player

digital camera

keyboard

video game handset

Peripherals · 4 · 12
A peripheral is any device that plugs into a computer or game console. Peripherals include the keyboard and mouse, as well as handsets.

CD burning · 11 · 16
CD-ROMs store data (information). Digital music files (or MP3s) can be put onto a CD using a CD burner. Most modern computers have built-in CD burners.

Handhelds ③ ⑦ ⑨

With small game consoles known as handhelds, people can play video games while on the move. Most handhelds take small cartridges, which store the information for individual games.

computer graphics

Games ⑥

Every year computer games become more and more complex and realistic, as computers become more powerful. Before home computers and game consoles, the games were played in video arcades.

Virtual reality ⑬ ⑭

Special headsets, gloves, and suits can allow people to experience virtual-reality games. These are computer programs that generate situations that look and feel virtually (almost) real.

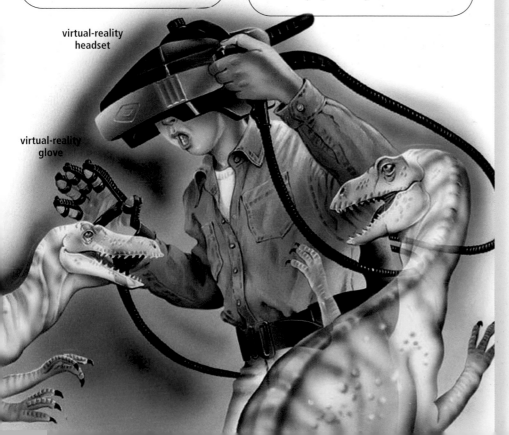

virtual-reality headset

virtual-reality glove

QUESTIONS:
Telephones

Level 1

1. What "T" is a written message sent by a cell phone?
2. Were the first cell phones bigger or smaller than cell phones today?
3. Do most modern telephones have rotating dials or buttons?
4. Do cell phones send messages using microwaves, water waves, or Mexican waves?
5. Are there cell phones that can connect to the Internet?

Level 2

6. Did the world's first telephone have touch-tone dialing?
7. In what century was the telephone invented: ninth, 19th, or 21st?
8. SAME CAR can be rearranged to spell what extra feature of some cell phones?
9. HOME CUT PIE can be rearranged to spell what part of a telephone that you speak into?
10. What "E" is the place where telephone calls are connected?
11. What name is given to the people who used to connect telephone calls?
12. How many names were in the first-ever telephone directory: 50, 500, or 5,000?
13. What "T" was a type of coded message used before telephones were invented?

Level 3

14. How did people generate the electricity to power early phones?
15. Who invented the telephone?
16. In which country was Alexander Graham Bell born?
17. Who invented the carbon-granule microphone?
18. Which was invented first: the fax machine or the telephone?
19. In what year did rotating dials appear: 1886, 1896, or 1906?

Telephones

The telephone is the world's most popular means of communication. Telephones connect friends and families all over the world and are a vital tool for most businesses. In recent years, the telephone has led to a new invention that has completely changed the world: the Internet.

Early years 14 17
Early telephones had handles that were wound in order to generate electricity to power them. In 1878 American Thomas Edison invented the carbon-granule microphone, which transmitted voices more clearly.

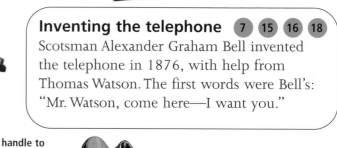

receiver

handle to generate electricity

earpiece on a wire

Inventing the telephone 7 15 16 18
Scotsman Alexander Graham Bell invented the telephone in 1876, with help from Thomas Watson. The first words were Bell's: "Mr. Watson, come here—I want you."

mouthpiece

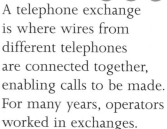

Dialing numbers 9 19
Rotating dials first appeared in 1896. Previously, people had to ask an operator to connect them. Early "candlestick" phones had earpieces on a wire and mouthpieces on top.

"candlestick" telephone

operators connecting calls

Exchanges 10 11 12
A telephone exchange is where wires from different telephones are connected together, enabling calls to be made. For many years, operators worked in exchanges. They connected calls by plugging wires into the correct sockets. Today most exchanges are automated. The first telephone directory was printed in 1878. It had only 50 names in it.

Modern phones ③ ⑥

Modern phones have touch-tone dialing. Each button generates its own sound, which is recognized by computers at the telephone exchange.

buttons

number pad sensors

electronic circuit board

inside the mouthpiece

screen

Telegrams ⑬ ⑱

Before telephones, people used telegrams— coded messages that were sent via wires and then decoded. The fax machine was invented in 1843.

Cellular phones ② ④

Cellular (cell) phones first became common in the 1980s. At first, they were around the size of a brick, but over time they got smaller. Cell phones send messages through the air using microwaves. Messages are collected by special masts and are then sent on to exchanges. They can then be transmitted via the masts or via fiber-optic cable to landline exchanges.

keypad

cell phone

BlackBerry

screen

11:35

New features ① ⑤ ⑧

Cell phones are changing all the time. As well as voice messages, most can transmit texts (typed messages) and even connect to the Internet and send e-mails. Many cell phones can be used for more than just communication. Some have built-in cameras, music, and video games.

QUESTIONS:
Discoveries

Level 1

1. What type of food is said to have fallen on Sir Isaac Newton's head, giving him the idea for his most famous theory?
2. What "W" turns around and around, allowing vehicles to move?
3. IT GRAVY can be rearranged to give the name of what force that pulls objects toward the ground?

Level 2

4. Which mathematician living in ancient Greece shouted, "Eureka!" when he was taking a bath?
5. What nationality was Sir Isaac Newton?
6. In which century did the first cars with gasoline engines appear?
7. Michael Faraday was an American scientist. True or false?
8. What "S" was used to power the earliest cars?
9. Karl Benz was a pioneer of the motorcar. True or false?
10. SPICY HITS can be rearranged to give the name of what type of scientist?
11. Who devised the theory of relativity?
12. Was the wheel invented more than 3,000 years ago?
13. What "M" did Michael Faraday help us understand better?
14. What nationality was Nicolas Cugnot, who built the first car?
15. By what three letters is deoxyribonucleic acid usually known?

Level 3

16. In which modern country are the ruins of the city of Uruk?
17. Which two scientists are usually credited with discovering the double helix of deoxyribonucleic acid?
18. In the formula $E = mc^2$, what does "E" stand for?

Discoveries

The history of science is a history of discoveries. The reason we know so much about the world is because of the great thinkers who had ideas and then tested them to see if they were true. Some of these ideas led to useful inventions. Others helped us better understand the universe around us.

Archimedes (4)

This ancient Greek made an important discovery about water displacement one day when he was in his bathtub and noticed water spilling out. At the moment the idea came to him, he shouted, "Eureka!"

The wheel (2) (12) (16)

Nobody knows who invented the wheel. The earliest images of wheels come from Iraq and date back around 5,500 years. At that time, a great civilization lived there, based around the city of Uruk. It is possible that the wheel was invented before this date, however.

Sir Isaac Newton

Faraday (7) (13)

Michael Faraday (1791–1867) was an English chemist and physicist who helped us understand the nature of electricity and magnetism.

Newton (1) (3) (5)

English scientist Sir Isaac Newton (1642–1727) discovered gravity. The idea came to him when he was sitting under a tree, and an apple fell on his head.

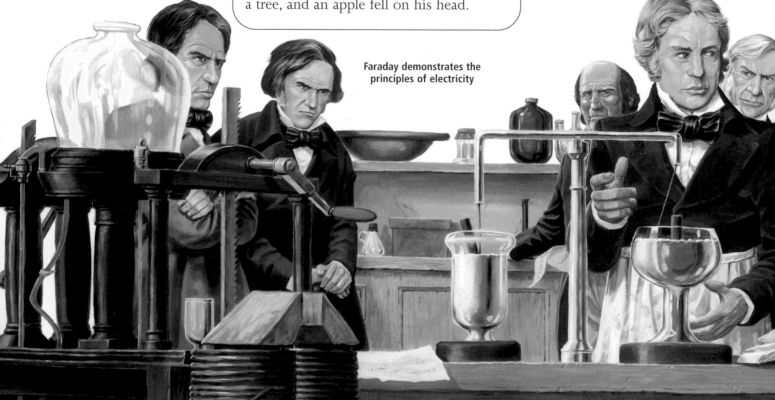

Faraday demonstrates the principles of electricity

The car ⑥ ⑧ ⑨ ⑭

The first self-propelled road vehicle was built by Frenchman Nicolas Cugnot in 1769 and was driven by steam. In the 1880s, Karl Benz and Gottlieb Daimler worked independently to produce the first gasoline engine. In 1885 Benz built his motorized three-wheel car, the first to be powered by gas.

Relativity ⑩ ⑪ ⑱

The theory of relativity was the brainchild of German-born physicist Albert Einstein (1879–1955). Einstein's theory showed that time, space, and mass are not fixed but change according to the position from which they are seen or measured. His theory also showed that mass and energy are interchangeable. He summed this up with a single equation: $E = mc^2$ ("E" is energy, "m" is mass, and "c^2" is acceleration).

the double helix

DNA ⑮ ⑰

All plants and animals contain molecules of DNA (deoxyribonucleic acid)—the blueprint for life. DNA consists of chains of paired units called bases. The structure of DNA, known as the double helix, was first described in 1953 by James Watson and Francis Crick.

QUESTIONS:
Where in the world?

Level 1

1. Is Cambridge in England or in Egypt?
2. Scissors were invented by Toshiba. True or false?
3. What "A" is an American computer company and also a piece of fruit?

Level 2

4. Was gunpowder invented in China, France, or Russia?
5. ARROW SLOPE can be rearranged to give the name of what form of power, used in Australia?
6. Is the company Sony from Europe, the United States, or Asia?
7. In which U.S. state is Silicon Valley: Kentucky, Vermont, or California?

Level 3

8. What "E" do Brazilian cars use instead of gasoline?
9. What "S" is the plant from which this fuel is extracted?
10. In which year did the first human heart transplant take place: 1967, 1977, or 1987?

Where in the world?

Advances in science and technology have caused changes all over the world. In some cases, they have made countries rich. In others, they have improved all of our lives. Every year scientists make new discoveries and inventors come up with new ideas and products. In 50 years' time, many more exciting advances will have completely changed the way that people live.

Japan 4 6
Asia has a long history of inventing. Gunpowder, for example, was invented in China. Today Japan is known for high-tech companies such as Sony, Toshiba, and Hitachi. Japanese car manufacturers Honda and Toyota are currently developing cars that use electricity instead of gas.

England 1
England's famous universities, Oxford and Cambridge, have been home to many groundbreaking scientists, including Sir Isaac Newton and Sir Stephen Hawkins.

Brazil 8 9
In Brazil, cars run on ethanol (alcohol) instead of gasoline. This protects the environment and uses up waste sugarcane, from which the ethanol is extracted.

NORTH AMERICA

EUROPE

ASIA

Egypt 2
Ancient Egypt produced many of the household objects that are common today, including paper and scissors.

AFRICA

AUSTRALASIA

SOUTH AMERICA

The United States 3 7
California is the home of Silicon Valley, where many of the world's biggest computer companies, such as Apple and Microsoft, have their headquarters.

South Africa 10
In 1967 Christiaan Barnard performed the first-ever human heart transplant in South Africa, revolutionizing the field of medicine.

Australia 5
With its baked outback and deserts, Australia is one of the world's biggest users of solar power. The country hosts a giant solar-powered car race every year, with teams from all over the world competing.

Answers 1) England **2)** False (they were invented in ancient Egypt) **3)** Apple **4)** China **5)** Solar power **6)** Asia **7)** California **8)** Ethanol **9)** Sugarcane **10)** 1967

QUIZ FOUR
History

QUESTIONS:
Ancient Egypt

Level 1

1. Which river flows through Egypt?
2. What did the ancient Egyptians call their leader?
3. Did Egyptians believe in life after death?
4. What was made of wool or human hair?
5. What were Egyptian clothes made from?

Level 2

6. What form of writing did the Egyptians use?
7. What was papyrus made from?
8. What was usually buried with an Egyptian's body?
9. How did the Egyptians usually decorate their coffins?
10. What was "Opening the Mouth"?
11. What is the biggest pyramid called?
12. What flower was the symbol of the Nile river?

Level 3

13. Which part of the body was used to measure a cubit: the leg, the foot, or the forearm?
14. How did the Egyptians transport a pharaoh's body?
15. What did Egyptians use to dry a body when embalming it?
16. What animal is associated with the Egyptian god of kings?
17. What did the priest say during a death ceremony?
18. For how long did the pharaohs rule Egypt?
19. Who is buried in the Great Pyramid of Giza?

More than 5,000 years ago, a great civilization was born on the banks of the Nile river in Egypt. Egyptians were ruled by one king, obeyed one set of laws, and worshipped one group of gods. Their civilization lasted for thousands of years. People's lives depended on the Nile, which overflowed each year and enriched the land.

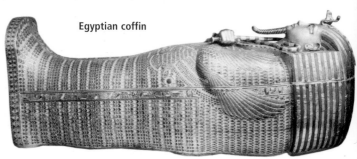

Egyptian coffin

Afterlife   3   8

The Egyptians believed that when a person died, they would live again in a kind of heaven. There, they needed the same things that they needed in Egypt, including their body. A person's clothes and furniture were buried in their tomb, together with food and drinks.

Writing   6   7

The Egyptians wrote on papyrus (paper made from reeds). They used red or black ink and a reed pen or a brush. Their writing consisted of pictures, called hieroglyphics, that stood for objects and sounds.

The Nile   1   12

The lotus blossom was the symbol of the Nile river in Egypt. Every year the river flooded its banks, leaving a layer of rich soil in which farmers grew crops.

Art   9

The Egyptians painted their coffins and the walls of their tombs beautifully. Each coffin was usually painted with a portrait of the dead person.

Pharaohs   2   16   18

The pharaohs (powerful kings) ruled Egypt for 3,000 years. The Egyptians believed that the pharaohs were gods, linked with Horus (the god of kings), who took the form of a hawk.

symbol of Horus

Mummies

15

After death, Egyptians preserved a body by embalming it. They used salt to dry the body and then wrapped it in linen. The head was covered with a mask.

Tombs

10 11 14 17 19

Pyramids were tombs for pharaohs. The largest is the Great Pyramid of Giza, built for the pharaoh Cheops (Khufu). The pharaoh's body was taken to his tomb in a funeral boat. Priests then performed a ceremony called "Opening the Mouth," saying, "You live again, you live again forever."

pharaoh's coffin on a funeral boat

Measurement

13

A cubit is 20.5 in. (52.5cm)—the average distance between a person's middle finger and their elbow. Egyptians made special rods to measure cubits exactly.

Clothes

4 5

Egyptians, even the pharaohs, usually walked barefoot or wore sandals made out of reeds. People wore simple linen clothes and sometimes wore wigs made of wool or human hair. Egyptians wore a lot of jewelry to keep away evil spirits.

wall painting of a duck

QUESTIONS: Ancient Greece

Level 1

1. What "M" is one of the seas around Greece?
2. Who was the ruler of the Greek gods?
3. Where were the ancient Olympic Games held?
4. Was the Trojan horse made out of stone or wood?
5. The Greeks had slaves. True or false?

Level 2

6. A SPRAT can be rearranged to give the name of what Greek city-state?
7. What did women use in order to weave fabrics for clothes?
8. At around what age did women get married?
9. Who hid inside the Trojan horse?
10. SNOOD PIE can be rearranged to give the name of which Greek god?
11. What material did the Greeks use to make bricks?
12. How did wealthy Greeks travel on land: by horse or by carriage?
13. The Greek Empire included many islands. True or false?
14. When traveling in Greece, people slept outside. True or false?
15. Where were the gods said to live?

Level 3

16. In which modern country was the ancient city of Troy?
17. What did a winner receive at the Olympic Games?
18. What was a *chiton*?
19. Where in a home did the Greeks have an altar?
20. Who was the goddess of the home?

Ancient Greece

The Greek civilization first emerged around 1200 B.C. and reached its height in around 500 B.C. The Greeks were the first people to introduce democracy, when men in Athens were given the right to vote. Many people were farmers, but a middle class of merchants and craftspeople emerged in the towns. The Greeks developed forms of philosophy, art, and architecture that have endured through the centuries.

Greece

Aegean Sea

Mediterranean Sea

Geography   1 6 13
Greece is surrounded by the Mediterranean and Aegean seas. The Greek Empire included city-states in Greece itself, such as Athens (the largest) and Sparta, and many islands.

Houses   5 11 19
Greek houses were made from mud bricks and wood. They were usually built around a courtyard, which contained an altar. There were separate quarters for men, women, and slaves.

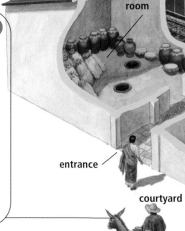

upstairs bedrooms

dining room

storage room

Traveling   12 14
On land, wealthy citizens traveled on horseback. Others walked. People often slept outside or on the porch of a public building when they were away from home.

entrance

altar

courtyard

store

Women's lives   7 8 18
Women got married at around 15. They looked after the household and used a loom to spin and weave fabrics. A single rectangular piece of cloth made a basic woman's dress, called a *chiton*.

Hermes   Diana   Zeus   Hera   Athena   Apollo

Greek gods
10 15 20

Greeks believed in many different gods, who represented every aspect of their lives: from music (Apollo) to love (Aphrodite); from the sea (Poseidon) to the home (Hestia). The gods were said to live on Mount Olympus, on the mainland of Greece.

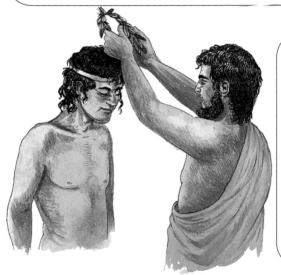

Olympic Games
2 3 17

The Olympics were held every four years at Olympia to honor Zeus, the ruler of the gods. Events included running and chariot races. The winner of each event was awarded with a crown of olive leaves.

Trojan horse
4 9 16

Troy was a city in what we now call Turkey. The Greeks wanted to capture Troy, so they presented the Trojans with a large wooden horse, in which some Greek soldiers were hiding. After nightfall, the soldiers left the horse and captured the city.

QUESTIONS:
The Colosseum

Level 1

1. What famous gladiator led a revolt of slaves?
2. There were elephants in the Colosseum. True or false?
3. What signal did the crowd give for a gladiator to die?
4. CUT ROSE can be rearranged to give the name of what type of gladiator?

Level 2

5. In what part of the Colosseum were the gladiators and animals kept?
6. Which emperor often fought at the Colosseum?
7. What was a *bestiarius*?
8. What did a *retiarius* use to catch his opponent?
9. Who were thrown to the animals?
10. What type of gladiator wore a helmet decorated with a fish?
11. How many years did it take to build the Colosseum: ten, 20, or 30?
12. The *venationes* were Roman soldiers. True or false?

Level 3

13. What did a freed gladiator receive?
14. How many people could attend games at the Colosseum?
15. When were the first gladiator games held?
16. How did the Colosseum get its name?
17. How many times did Commodus fight at the Colosseum?
18. How many animals were killed in the first celebrations at the Colosseum?

FIND THE ANSWER: The Colosseum

The ancient Romans built huge arenas called amphitheaters to stage their entertainment. The Colosseum in Rome was one of the grandest, commissioned by Emperor Vespasian. The first ceremonies lasted for 100 days and included a mock sea battle. Romans enjoyed watching bloodthirsty games at the Colosseum for more than 400 years.

Punishment 7 9
Christians, criminals, and slaves were thrown into the arena with wild animals. The *bestiarius*, on the other hand, was trained to fight animals.

Gladiators 3 15
The first gladiator games were held in 264 B.C. Most gladiators were prisoners, slaves, or criminals who were trained to fight. If a gladiator was wounded, the crowd decided his fate by giving the thumbs up (to live) or the thumbs down (to die).

gladiator's helmet

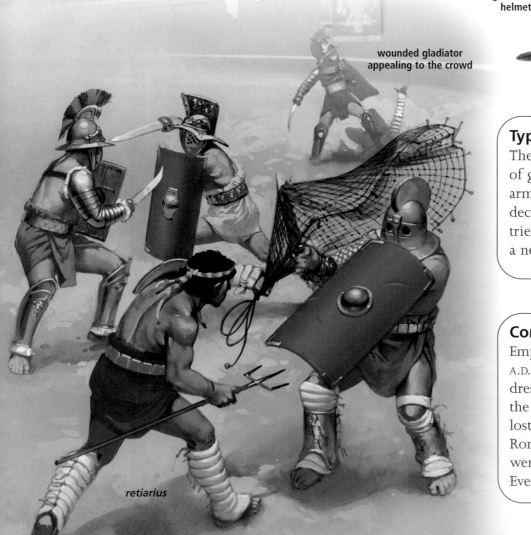
wounded gladiator appealing to the crowd

retiarius

Types of gladiators 4 8 10
There were several different types of gladiators. The *secutor* was heavily armed. The *murmillo* wore a helmet decorated with a fish. The *retiarius* tried to catch his opponent with a net and a three-pronged spear.

Commodus 6 17
Emperor Commodus reigned from A.D. 180–192. During his reign, he dressed as a gladiator and fought at the Colosseum 735 times. He never lost. This behavior shocked many Romans, who thought that gladiators were the lowest members of society. Eventually, Commodus was murdered.

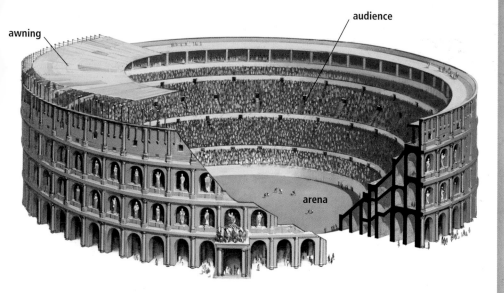

awning

audience

arena

QUESTIONS:
Medieval life

Level 1

1. A banquet is a type of battle. True or false?
2. People ate meals in the great hall. True or false?
3. Was a jongleur a person or a musical instrument?
4. Who owned the land in medieval times?
5. Who taught the children of noblemen: priests or servants?

Level 2

6. Who rented land from noblemen?
7. What were jongleurs called in England?
8. What was the name of the system by which land was given out?
9. What was the center of a castle called?
10. Where did important people sit during a banquet?
11. How were castle floors kept warm?
12. Where were medieval girls taught?
13. What was the cup board for?
14. What was used to help rid the castle floor of bad smells?

Level 3

15. What language did the sons of nobles learn?
16. Why did people like to hear music while they were eating?
17. Where did village boys learn trades?
18. What were trenchers?

The Colosseum 5 11 14 16
It took around ten years to build the Colosseum, which got its name from the nearby colossus (statue) of Nero. It had 80 entrances and was divided into the podium, arena, and *cavea* (seating area) for 50,000 people. Underground chambers held gladiators and animals.

Spartacus 1
Spartacus, a Thracian soldier, was sold into slavery and became a gladiator in Capua. In 73 B.C., Spartacus led a revolt of slaves, but he was eventually defeated and killed.

Exotic animals 2 12 18
Venationes (staged hunts) were held in the morning. Exotic animals, such as elephants and tigers, were imported from overseas. During the first shows at the Colosseum, 5,000 animals were killed.

bone tablet and coins

Freedom 13
If a gladiator fought well, he could be set free. His master gave him a bone tablet, inscribed with his name, and a gift of coins.

FIND THE ANSWER: Medieval life

Society in the Middle Ages was strictly ordered. The king, at the head, owned all of the land but allowed certain noblemen to use it in return for their loyalties and services in war. Peasants led difficult lives and had few rights. Social events were important for all medieval people—lords held banquets in their castles, while villagers attended weddings and fairs.

traveling musicians

The great hall   2 10 13 18
People dined and were entertained in the great hall. The lord and other important people sat at a "high table" near a display of cups and plates on the "cup board" that showed off the lord's wealth. Diners ate off wooden boards called trenchers.

Music   3 7 16
Traveling musicians, called jongleurs in France and gleemen in England, entertained guests by singing and playing musical instruments such as the lute and the harp. People believed that music aided digestion.

Banquets   1
Banquets (feasts) were held to show a lord's generosity and wealth, as well as for celebration. Food included beef, lamb, venison, fish, cheeses, eggs, bread, vegetables, and fruits, as well as wines and ales. Lavish banquets included figs, dates, and citrus fruits.

spiral staircase

bedchambers

The castle (9) (11) (14)

A spiral staircase led to the main tower, which was used for defense. The center of the castle, the keep, held the great hall, kitchen, chapel, and upstairs bedchambers. The stone floors were covered with reeds for warmth and were sprinkled with spices to reduce bad smells.

great hall

priest teaching sons of nobles

Learning (5) (12) (15) (17)

Children of nobles were taught by priests. They learned grammar, logic, Latin, and mathematics. Village boys learned trades, such as masonry (stonework), at local guilds, while girls were taught cooking and sewing at home.

Feudal system (4) (6) (8)

In feudal society, the king, who owned the land, granted fiefs of land to nobles. This land was then rented by the knights and lords, who had peasants farm it. The peasants, or serfs, were allowed to farm a small area to feed their families.

QUESTIONS:
Knights

Level 1

1. What "L" was a weapon used by knights on horseback?
2. What was a battering ram used for?
3. RED GAG can be rearranged to give the name of what weapon used by knights?
4. Knights only ever fought on horseback. True or false?

Level 2

5. What did an esquire become during a dubbing ceremony?
6. What was a mace?
7. How did a jousting knight knock his opponent off his horse?
8. What type of missiles did a mangonel shoot?
9. Did a knight use a crossbow or a longbow?
10. Why did jousting begin?
11. What weapon was used to shoot bolts at a castle?
12. How could knights tell each other apart in battle?
13. What is a trebuchet?
14. How could attackers force the defenders of a castle to surrender?

Level 3

15. What was the name of the fee paid by knights who did not want to fight?
16. What was a bevor?
17. How was an esquire dubbed?
18. By which century had knights begun wearing plated armor?

FIND THE ANSWER: Knights

Knights were sons of noblemen who trained to become soldiers of the king. A knight began training as a page at the age of seven. He then became an esquire, an assistant to a knight, before finally becoming a knight himself at the age of 21. Knights were bound by the rules of chivalry and fought to the death to protect their king and country.

Jousting   7 10
Although it began as battle training, jousting became popular entertainment to show off knights' skills at riding and fighting. Pairs of knights used dull lances to try to knock their opponent off his horse.

Armor   16 18
By the 1400s, knights wore plated armor, which offered better protection than mail armor. Large metal plates were joined by smaller plates called lames. The knight's neck was protected by a bevor, which was attached to the breastplate.

defenders with bows

scaling ladders

Dubbing   5 17
Esquires became knights in a ceremony called dubbing. The knight's lord tapped him on the shoulder with the flat blade of his sword.

Defense   14
Defenders shot arrows from window slits and threw rocks, boiling water, and red-hot irons at the enemy. Many sieges ended when the defenders were starved into surrendering.

Siege weapons 8 11 13

A trebuchet hurled stones at castle walls. A ballista, like a giant crossbow, shot bolts. The mangonel was a catapult used for throwing rocks.

trebuchet

ballista

mangonel

Battle 1 4 12 15

Knights fought on horseback with lances and on foot with other weapons. A knight was identified by the coat of arms he wore on his surcoat. Knights who did not want to fight had to pay a scutage fee to the king.

broadsword

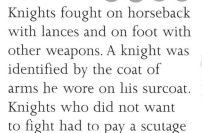

mace

crossbow

dagger

shield

ax

longbow

Weaponry 3 6 9

A knight's weapons included a crossbow, ax, mace (heavy club), longbow, broadsword, dagger, and a shield.

Castle siege 2

Attackers used battering rams and catapults to weaken castle walls. They also tunneled under the castle and shot at it from a siege tower. Meanwhile, archers on the ground kept a steady stream of arrows aimed at the defenders.

siege tower

siege catapult

QUESTIONS:
The Renaissance

Level 1

1. Does the word "Renaissance" mean "rebirth" or "revolting"?
2. BLAMER can be rearranged to give the name of what material used by Renaissance sculptors?
3. Was Donatello a painter or a sculptor?
4. The lute is a musical instrument. True or false?

Level 2

5. Ghiberti was a Renaissance philosopher. True or false?
6. Where was block printing invented?
7. What was the *lira da braccio* used for?
8. What painting featured the ancient philosophers Plato and Aristotle?
9. What was the first-ever mass-produced book?
10. HARE PAL can be rearranged to give the name of what Renaissance artist?
11. What nationality was Erasmus?
12. Which two civilizations influenced Renaissance artists?
13. What is the name of the leather pad that applied the ink in the first European printing press?
14. What type of philosophers thought that moral lessons could be learned from ancient texts?

Level 3

15. What "B" was a famous Renaissance architect?
16. In what year was the printing press invented in Europe?
17. The Renaissance lasted until which century?
18. Who invented the printing press in Europe?

The Renaissance

The Renaissance was an era of great change that brought Europe out of the Middle, or Dark, Ages. It began in the 1300s in the Italian cities of Florence and Venice and later spread across Europe. Artists, musicians, architects, and thinkers flourished with the support of wealthy patrons such as the Medici family. Fine libraries, academies, and universities were established.

psaltery

lira da braccio

Music 4 7
Renaissance instruments included the psaltery and the *lira da braccio*, used by poets to accompany their poems. The lute, the recorder, and the *organetto*, which used pipes, were also popular.

Ideas 1 11 14 17
"Renaissance" means "rebirth." There was a reawakened interest in science, art, and literature. The period lasted until the 1600s. Humanism was one important movement. Humanists, such as the Dutch philosopher Erasmus, thought moral lessons could be learned from Greek and Latin texts.

Painting 8 10 12
Artists were drawn to the human form, nature, and the art of ancient Greece and Rome. Raphael painted Greek philosophers like Aristotle and Plato in *The School of Athens*.

bronze sculpture

Renaissance artists

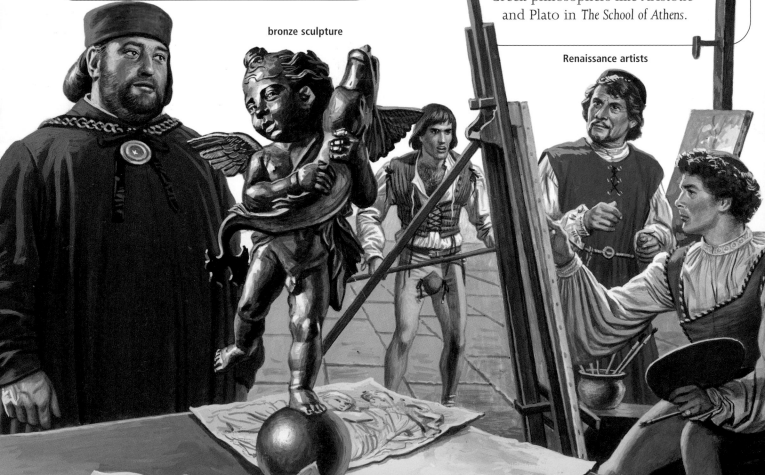

Sculpture

Sculptors, such as Donatello and Ghiberti, created amazingly realistic work that was inspired by classical sculptures, although they did not necessarily depict classical themes. Donatello carved saints and prophets clothed in Roman or Greek styles. Sculptors used materials such as bronze and marble.

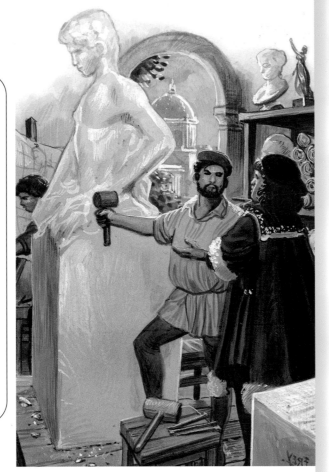

classical-style arch

Architecture

Early Italian architects, such as Brunelleschi and Palladio, looked to classical styles for their designs, using Greek columns and Roman arches on many buildings.

Inventions

Block printing was invented in China, but Johannes Gutenberg, a German, invented the printing press in Europe in 1440. It had moveable type held in a wooden frame, and ink was applied using a leather pad called an "inkball." In 1455 Gutenberg printed a Bible that became the world's first-ever mass-produced book.

Gutenberg's printing press

QUESTIONS:
The age of exploration

Level 1

1. Was Sir Francis Drake an Englishman or a Spaniard?
2. What was Columbus' largest ship called: the *Santa Maria*, the *Santa Anna*, or the *Santa Barbara*?
3. Francisco Pizarro conquered the Incas. True or false?
4. From which country was Bartholomew Dias?

Level 2

5. Which did Magellan discover: the Indian Ocean or the Pacific Ocean?
6. How many men were in the crew of Columbus' largest ship: 30, 40, or 60?
7. Who sent Columbus to find a route to China?
8. Did Dias or da Gama sail around the southern tip of Africa?
9. Who reached India in 1498?
10. What was Zheng He the first to do?
11. What were the names of Columbus' two caravels?
12. What was a back staff used for?
13. Why did Ferdinand Magellan not reach his final destination?
14. What did Columbus believe he had reached?
15. What part of the world did the Incas rule?

Level 3

16. On which island did Columbus land?
17. What was discovered in 1911?
18. What is a *nao*?
19. When did a ship first sail all the way around the world?

The age of exploration

During the 1400s and 1500s, Europeans became increasingly curious about the world. Explorers made bold strides in their efforts to increase trade, find wealth, and discover new worlds. By the end of this era, Portuguese, Spanish, and English explorers had made their way to Africa, India, China, America, and around the globe.

compass

Navigation 10 12

Compasses, star charts, and back staffs, which measured the angle of the Sun, helped explorers find their way. Zheng He was the first person to use a compass on his sea voyages.

Columbus 7 14 16

Christopher Columbus was sent by the Spanish king to find a route to China. When Columbus arrived at the Caribbean island of San Salvador in 1492, he thought that he had reached the Far East.

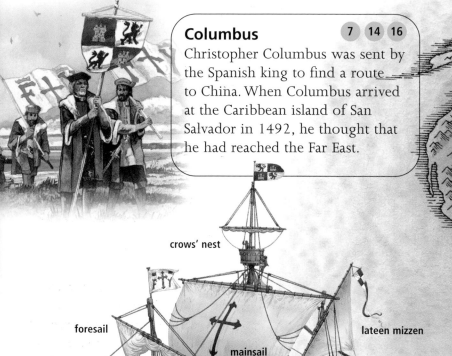

crows' nest

foresail

mainsail

lateen mizzen

quarterdeck

forecastle

steerage

hold

NORTH AMERICA

SOUTH AMERICA

Key
Dias's route
······ da Gama's route
Magellan's route
Columbus' route
Drake's route

Ships 2 6 11 18

Christopher Columbus' largest ship was the *Santa Maria*, a *nao*, or merchant ship, usually used for cargo. The others, called the *Niña* and the *Pinta*, were caravels, which were much lighter ships. The *Santa Maria* held a crew of 40 men and had large square sails that gave it a lot of power at sea.

Great exploration routes 1 4 8 9

In 1488 Portuguese explorer Bartholomew Dias sailed around the southern tip of Africa. In 1497–1498 Vasco da Gama traveled to India. One hundred years later, Sir Francis Drake, an Englishman, traveled around the world.

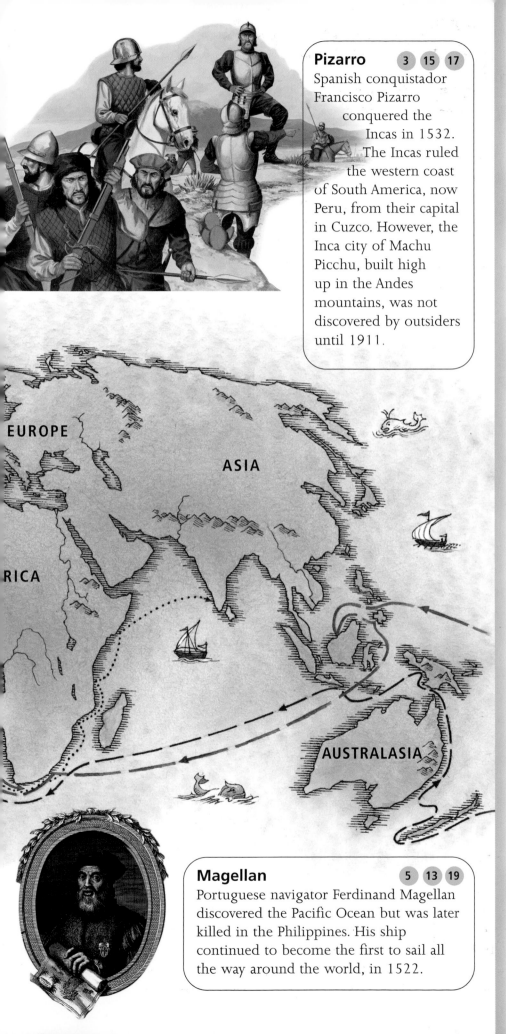

Pizarro ③ ⑮ ⑰
Spanish conquistador Francisco Pizarro conquered the Incas in 1532. The Incas ruled the western coast of South America, now Peru, from their capital in Cuzco. However, the Inca city of Machu Picchu, built high up in the Andes mountains, was not discovered by outsiders until 1911.

EUROPE

ASIA

RICA

AUSTRALASIA

Magellan ⑤ ⑬ ⑲
Portuguese navigator Ferdinand Magellan discovered the Pacific Ocean but was later killed in the Philippines. His ship continued to become the first to sail all the way around the world, in 1522.

QUESTIONS:
World War I

Level 1

1. What large machine was used for the first time in World War I?
2. What is a dogfight?
3. What was the area between enemy trenches called?
4. A grenade is a weapon. True or false?

Level 2

5. What type of protection did soldiers have against gas?
6. For what purpose were horses used?
7. Which "J" was a major battle fought at sea?
8. Where was the Western Front?
9. What name is used for a trained marksman who tries to shoot lone soldiers?
10. What weapon could be attached to a rifle?
11. How many lives were lost in the war: more than 7.5 million, more than 8.5 million, or more than ten million?
12. In which country is Jutland?
13. What lined the tops of trenches?
14. What weapons were installed in fighter planes?

Level 3

15. In what year was poison gas first used?
16. Which model of tank was the first one strong enough to withstand antitank rifles?
17. What was the name given to the British soldiers who trained horses?
18. What German fighter plane was considered to be the best fighter plane of the war?

FIND THE ANSWER: World War I

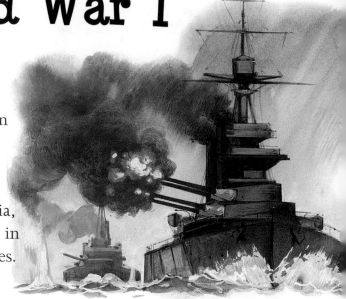

World War I, often called "The Great War," was thought to be the "war to end all wars." The war began with the assassination of Archduke Francis Ferdinand in 1914. The Central Powers of Germany, Bulgaria, Austro-Hungary, and Turkey fought against the Allied forces, which included Great Britain, France, and Russia, as well as a number of other countries. The war ended in 1918 when the Central Powers surrendered to the Allies.

British Mark IV tank

Tanks   1   16
During World War I, tanks were used for the first time in battle. The British Mark IV, introduced in 1918, was the first tank that was strong enough to withstand antitank rifles.

Battle of Jutland   7   12
The largest sea battle fought during World War I occurred in the North Sea near Jutland, Denmark. Both the Allies and the Central Powers claimed that they had won.

The Western Front   8   11
Fighting was the fiercest in the trenches, built through Belgium and France and known as the Western Front. The war claimed more than 8.5 million lives.

Trench warfare   3   13
Trench systems were made up of interconnecting dugouts. The land between the two opposing trenches was called no-man's-land. The tops of the trenches were lined with sandbags to absorb enemy fire. Soldiers in the muddy, cold, and unsanitary trenches suffered from trench foot, dysentery, and body lice.

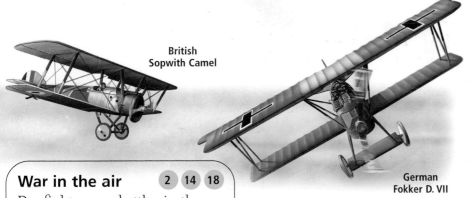

British
Sopwith Camel

German
Fokker D. VII

War in the air   2   14   18
Dogfights were battles in the air between two or more aircraft with machine guns. The German Fokker D. VII was considered to be the best fighter plane of the war.

Poison gas   5   15
Poison gas was used for the first time in 1915 in Ypres (Ieper, Belgium). Although soldiers had masks for protection, more than 90,000 men died from the poison.

soldier
wearing a
gas mask

Horses   6   17
British soldiers called "roughriders" trained tough horse breeds, such as the Australian Waler, to haul ambulances and weapons.

Snipers   9
Snipers were trained marksmen who looked for movement in the enemy trenches, trying to shoot lone soldiers.

Weapons   4   10
Grenades are bombs thrown by hand. Soldiers were also supplied with bayonets, short blades that could be attached to rifles. These were used in close combat.

bayonet

rifle

QUESTIONS:
Where in the world?

Level 1
1. What type of ruler led the Chinese?
2. In which continent did the ancient Romans live?
3. What were Japanese warriors called?

Level 2
4. In which continent was the Shona Empire?
5. Which European people settled in Argentina?
6. Where did the Iroquois live?
7. Which empire ruled Australia by 1829?

Level 3
8. For what is Mansa Musa famous?
9. What trading route did Chinese traders use to reach the West?
10. Which people were the first to use writing?

FIND THE ANSWER: Where in the world?

Every inhabited continent in the world has a rich history. Hunter-gatherers moved from place to place in search of food and shelter until settlements were established. Great empires rose and fell. In the meantime, people lived, traveled, invented, built, fought wars, and sought peace. They left behind great art, monuments, and ways of thinking that are still fascinating today.

Asia 1 3 9

The Chinese were ruled by emperors. Powerful dynasties (successions of leaders from one family) were established. Chinese traders took goods along the Silk Road, a trading route to the West. In Japan, warriors called samurai ruled the land on behalf of their emperor.

North America 6
Before the Europeans arrived, Native Americans like the Iroquois lived by hunting and farming. European settlers won their independence from the British in 1776 and formed the United States.

Europe 2
The ancient Greeks and Romans were among the first European civilizations. Years later, the British, Spanish, Dutch, French, and Portuguese colonized other parts of the world and created new empires.

The Middle East 10
The Sumerians were the first to use writing. Later the Assyrians and Persians ruled the area, fighting battles to expand their empires.

Africa 4 8
The oldest human history begins in Africa. In the south, Great Zimbabwe was the capital of the Shona Empire. In the west, Mansa Musa built the great trading city of Timbuktu in Mali.

South America 5
South America was populated by scattered tribes until the 1500s, when the Portuguese settled in Brazil and the Spaniards in Argentina.

Australasia 7
The Polynesians were among the first explorers. Aborigines lived on the mainland. By 1829, Australia was part of the British Empire.

NORTH AMERICA

SOUTH AMERICA

EUROPE

ASIA

AFRICA

AUSTRALASIA

Answers 1) An emperor **2)** Europe **3)** Samurai **4)** Africa **5)** The Spanish **6)** North America **7)** The British Empire **8)** He built Timbuktu **9)** The Silk Road **10)** The Sumerians

Sports and art

QUESTIONS:
Summer Olympics

Level 1

1. How many rings are there in the Olympic symbol?
2. Which Olympic sport features a 16-ft. (5-m)-long springy pole?
3. How often are the Summer Olympic Games held?
4. Do equestrian events use a horse, a bicycle, or a pistol?
5. Which type of swimming race is longer: a sprint or an endurance race?

Level 2

6. Is a marathon race 20km, 42km, or 50km long?
7. What is the name of a competitor in a judo fight?
8. Which horse-based sport takes three days to complete?
9. What is the name of the building in which track cyclists compete?
10. Who set a world record of 6.14m for the pole vault?
11. What is the longest distance race in track events at the Olympics?
12. How many Olympics has Jeannie Longo-Ciprelli appeared at: three, four, or six?
13. In which sport did Mark Spitz win seven gold medals in 1972?

Level 3

14. How long is a steeplechase race at the Olympics?
15. When was judo first included in the Olympics?
16. How much shorter is a woman's judo bout than a man's?
17. What fraction of the total gold medals for judo did Japan win in 2004?

Summer Olympics

First held in 1896, the modern Summer Olympic Games are the biggest multisports event in the world. The Games are watched by hundreds of millions of people on television all around the world. Thousands of athletes compete in sports as varied as shooting, high diving, and fencing. Their goal is to be the best in the world and win a highly prized gold medal.

Olympic flag   1
In 1913 the founder of the Olympics, Baron Pierre de Coubertin, unveiled the five-ring symbol of the Olympics.

Equestrian events   4   8
Equestrian events were introduced in 1912 for horses and riders. Horses race in show jumping around a course of obstacles. Eventing is held over three days.

Running   6   11   14
Track includes all of the running and racewalking events. The shortest is the 100m sprint. The longest are the 42km marathon and 50km racewalk. Runners jump over hurdles in the 100m, 110m, and 400m races. There are barriers to clear in the 3,000m steeplechase.

show jumping

pistol shooting

running

swimming

Cycling   9   12
Events include mountain biking and track cycling in a velodrome. Frenchwoman Jeannie Longo-Ciprelli is famous for cycling in six Olympics.

Swimming   5   13   16
In the 50m-long Olympic swimming pool the events range from 50m sprints to 1,500m endurance races. American swimmer Mark Spitz won seven gold medals for swimming at the 1972 Games.

Hosts

3

Every four years, cities bid for the right to host the Summer Olympics. Sydney, Australia, staged the 2000 Games and Athens, Greece, the 2004 games. In 2008 they will be held in Beijing, China, and, in 2012, London, England.

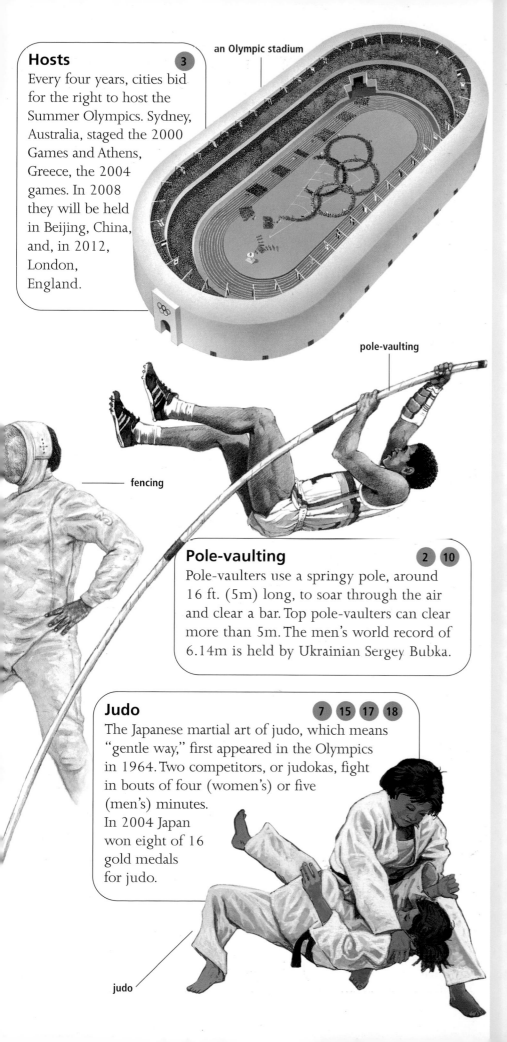

an Olympic stadium

fencing

pole-vaulting

Pole-vaulting

2 **10**

Pole-vaulters use a springy pole, around 16 ft. (5m) long, to soar through the air and clear a bar. Top pole-vaulters can clear more than 5m. The men's world record of 6.14m is held by Ukrainian Sergey Bubka.

Judo

7 **15** **17** **18**

The Japanese martial art of judo, which means "gentle way," first appeared in the Olympics in 1964. Two competitors, or judokas, fight in bouts of four (women's) or five (men's) minutes. In 2004 Japan won eight of 16 gold medals for judo.

judo

QUESTIONS:
Gymnastics

Level 1
1. When do athletes warm up?
2. What are people who perform gymnastics called?
3. How many handles does a pommel horse have?
4. Are the rings used only by men or by both men and women?
5. What do some athletes dust their hands with to help with their grip?

Level 2
6. In gymnastics, how many events do female athletes compete in?
7. Did rhythmic gymnastics first appear in the Olympics in 1932, 1968, or 1984?
8. How many items of equipment are there in rhythmic gymnastics?
9. Was the first person to get the highest possible score in artistic gymnastics at the Olympics a man or a woman?
10. What is the highest possible score given to a competitor for one routine: 10, 15, or 20?
11. What "H" is a piece of rhythmic gymnastics equipment?
12. What are the two hoops that hang above the ground called?
13. What type of gymnastics is performed to music?
14. How many panels of judges score rhythmic gymnastics?

Level 3
15. How high are the parallel bars?
16. Who was the first person to get the highest possible score in artistic gymnastics at the Olympics?
17. Who invented the parallel bars?
18. From which gymnastics apparatus would a gymnast dismount?

Gymnastics

Gymnastics is a sport in which people perform a series of movements that require strength, balance, and flexibility. Artistic gymnasts perform moves on apparatus such as the parallel bars, rings, and the pommel horse. Rhythmic gymnastics is a combination of gymnastics moves and dance.

men's leather hand guard

women's leather hand guard

chalk

Get a grip   5

Many gymnasts dust their hands with chalk, which helps them get a strong grip on the apparatus that they are using. Some also wear leather hand protectors to prevent sprains and injuries.

Pommel horse   2 3 18

The pommel horse has two handles on top. The gymnast (someone who performs gymnastics) carries out a series of swinging moves before leaving the pommel horse and landing. This is called the dismount.

asymmetric bars

balance bea

pommel horse

floor mat

vaulting horse

horizontal bar

the rings

parallel bars

scoreboards

judges

Rings   4 12

This event is only for male gymnasts. The athlete swings on two rings, which hang 9 ft. (2.75m) above a mat on the floor. They need a lot of strength to perform their moves on the rings.

Judging   6 9 10 16

In artistic gymnastics, men are judged in six events and women in four. In 1976 Nadia Comaneci became the first to achieve the highest score of 10.

Rhythmic gymnastics   7   13   14

Rhythmic gymnasts have been perfoming in the Olympics since 1984. Their routines are performed to music, last between 60 and 120 seconds, and are scored by three panels of judges.

Equipment   8   11

Rhythmic gymnasts use five pieces of equipment in their routines: a pair of clubs, a ribbon, a rope, a ball, and a hoop.

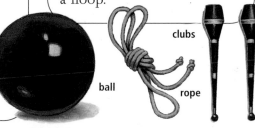

ball

rope

clubs

Parallel bars   15   17

Invented by Friedrich Jahn, the two flexible parallel bars stand 5. 7 ft. (1.75m) high and between 16–20 in. (42–52cm) apart. They are used by male gymnasts, who swing and then perform handstands and one-arm moves on them.

Warming up   1

Gymnasts always warm up before competing. The warm-up stretches their muscles so that they perform their best and helps prevent injuries from occurring.

QUESTIONS: Winter sports

Level 1

1. How many skis does a skier use?
2. Do speed skaters race downhill, around a track, or along a road?
3. Which country invented ice hockey?
4. Which is also known as cross-country skiing: Nordic or downhill?
5. What name is given to someone who teaches others how to ski?

Level 2

6. In which winter sport do players try to hit a puck into a goal?
7. What is the front of a snowboard called?
8. Downhill skiing is part of the Winter Olympics. True or false?
9. What is the name of the sticks that skiers hold in their hands?
10. In which winter sport can competitors reach a speed of 37 mph (60km/h) as they race around a track?
11. Are there six, nine, or 11 players per team in ice hockey?
12. Do Nordic or slalom skiers race a zigzagging course?
13. What is the back of a snowboard called?
14. How many periods are there in an ice hockey game?
15. The biathlon involves rifle shooting and what type of skiing?
16. In what year did snowboarding become an Olympic sport?

Level 3

17. Who can travel the fastest: speed skaters or downhill skiers?
18. What object attaches ski boots to skis?
19. Which skis are shorter and wider: Nordic skis or downhill skis?
20. What is the name of the player who guards a goal in ice hockey?

Winter sports

downhill skier in action

Winter sports all involve snow or ice—and sometimes both. They can be a lot of fun to try out, and most are also competitive sports. Many winter sports, such as skiing and skating, have developed out of people's need to travel through snow and ice. People have been ice-skating, for example, for more than 3,000 years.

Downhill skiing `8` `12` `17`

Downhill skiing is one of the most exciting sports in the Winter Olympics. Skiers can sometimes reach speeds of more than 80 mph (130km/h) in competitions. Slalom skiing is a version of downhill skiing. Competitors must zigzag around a course as fast as possible.

Learning how to ski `1` `5` `9` `18`

Millions of people learn how to ski every year on gentle ski slopes or artificial dry slopes. Teachers are called ski instructors. Skiers wear special boots that attach to their two skis with clips called bindings. They use ski poles to push themselves forward.

Nordic skiing `4` `15` `19`

Nordic, or cross-country, skiers travel long distances across gentle slopes and level surfaces. They use skis that are longer and narrower than downhill ones. In competitions, a top skier may complete a 9 mi. (15km) course in less than 50 minutes. Some Nordic skiers also take part in the biathlon, which combines Nordic skiing and rifle shooting.

Nordic skiing in Finland

Snowboarding 7 13 16

Snowboarding became an Olympic sport in 1998. In freestyle snowboarding, riders perform tricks similar to skateboarding. They press down on the back, or tail, of the board to lift the front, or nose, and perform jumps and other exciting moves.

a snowboarder performs a trick

Ice hockey 3 6 11 14 20

Ice hockey was invented in Canada. The six-player teams skate on the ice and score points by hitting a puck past the goalkeeper into a goal. Ice hockey is played in three 20-minute-long periods.

Speed skating 2 10 17

Skating can be fun—and a serious sport. Speed skaters race around icy tracks at speeds of 37 mph (60km/h). Figure skaters are judged on their routines of skating moves.

skating in a city park

QUESTIONS:
Baseball

Level 1

1. Baseball gloves are made out of cotton. True or false?
2. How many bases are there on a baseball field: four, 14, or 20?
3. A changeup is a type of baseball bat. True or false?
4. Does the catcher stand just behind the batter or just in front of him?

Level 2

5. Which is covered in dirt: the infield or the outfield?
6. What "M" is a piece of baseball equipment worn on the hand?
7. People played baseball in the 1800s. True or false?
8. Is Yankee Stadium in San Francisco, New York City, or Los Angeles?
9. MOTEL HEAP can be rearranged to give the name of which place on a baseball field?
10. Who would "bunt" a ball: a batter, a pitcher, or a fielder?
11. What "F" is a type of baseball pitch, thrown fast?
12. Which player wears a mask made out of metal?
13. What baseball team plays at Fenway Park?
14. How far away does the pitcher stand from the batter: 60.5 ft. (18m), 70.5 ft. (21m), or 80.5 ft. (25m)?

Level 3

15. In what town is Abner Doubleday said to have invented baseball?
16. In which stadium do the St. Louis Cardinals play?

FIND THE ANSWER:  Baseball

Baseball is known as the U.S.'s national pastime and is played mostly during the summer months. The sport is also played in Canada, South America, and Japan. However, the top professionals play in the American Major Leagues, where 30 teams compete each season for baseball's ultimate prize, the World Series.

Early baseball 7 15

Professional baseball began in North America in 1871. Legend has it that the game was invented by soldier Abner Doubleday in Cooperstown, New York, in 1839. In fact, the sport had been popular since the early 1800s.

19th-century game of baseball

The batter 2 9

The batter stands at home plate. He can score a home run if he rounds all four bases without the ball being caught by the opposing team (an "out").

catcher

home plate

The pitcher 14

The pitcher throws the ball to the batter from the pitcher's mound, which is 60.5 ft. (18.4m) from home plate. He must keep one foot in contact with the "pitcher's rubber" on the center of the mound at all times. Some pitchers can throw the ball at more than 100 mph (161km/h).

The catcher 4 12

The catcher squats behind the batter and signals to the pitcher what type of pitch to throw. He is heavily protected by a metal mask, shin and knee guards, and a padded chest guard.

metal mask

catcher's mitt

shin guard

fielder's glove

bat

first base mitt

baseball

Equipment 1 6

Baseball bats are usually made out of wood. The ball has a hard core, surrounded by yarn and covered with two pieces of horsehide stitched together. Gloves and mitts are made out of leather.

catcher's mitt

Batting   3 10 11

A batter must be ready for any type of pitch. The most common is the fastball, thrown straight and fast. A changeup is a slow pitch, intended to confuse the batter. Sometimes batters will gently tap the ball ("bunt" it), instead of swinging.

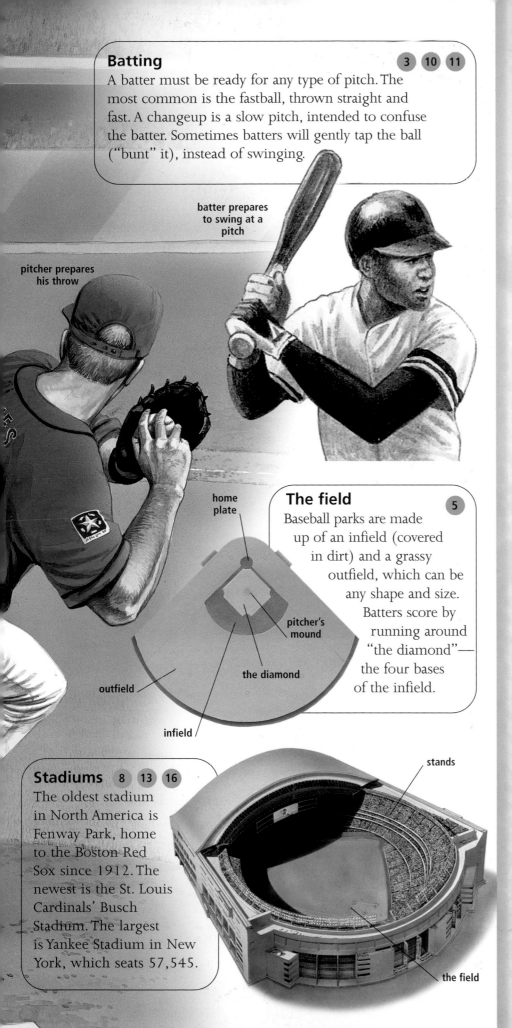

batter prepares to swing at a pitch

pitcher prepares his throw

The field   5

Baseball parks are made up of an infield (covered in dirt) and a grassy outfield, which can be any shape and size. Batters score by running around "the diamond"— the four bases of the infield.

home plate

pitcher's mound

the diamond

outfield

infield

Stadiums   8 13 16

The oldest stadium in North America is Fenway Park, home to the Boston Red Sox since 1912. The newest is the St. Louis Cardinals' Busch Stadium. The largest is Yankee Stadium in New York, which seats 57,545.

stands

the field

QUESTIONS:
Art and painting

Level 1

1. The famous artist Michelangelo came from Italy. True or false?
2. What was van Gogh's first name?
3. In what country are the famous Lascaux cave paintings?
4. Were sculptures, cave paintings, or frescoes made on damp plaster?
5. The Lascaux cave paintings feature paintings of reindeer. True or false?

Level 2

6. What part of an egg was used by prehistoric cave painters?
7. Can you name either of the colors that were often used by the ancient Greeks to decorate their pottery?
8. Do artists who paint frescoes have to work slowly or quickly?
9. Does tempera or oil paint produce richer colors?
10. Did Michelangelo paint a fresco on the doors, the walls, or the ceiling of the Sistine Chapel?
11. From what was Michelangelo's sculpture of Moses carved?
12. Does oil paint or tempera paint dry more slowly?
13. What part of an egg was used to make tempera paints?

Level 3

14. *Blam!* is a famous pop art painting. Who painted it?
15. In what century did Michelangelo carve a sculpture of Moses?
16. How old was van Gogh when he painted *Starry Night*?
17. In which decade did pop art first appear?
18. Are the prehistoric paintings in the Lascaux caves around 15,000, 16,000, or 17,000 years old?

FIND THE ANSWER: Art and painting

Art is any piece of creative work that is used to portray images and express feelings. People have been making art for tens of thousands of years. Art is produced in many different forms, including photography, drawing, and sculpture. Painting is one type of art that has been performed for at least 30,000 years.

Cave painting 3 5 18

The most famous early paintings were discovered in 1940 in the Lascaux caves in France. The lifelike animal paintings include horses, reindeer, oxen, and bulls. They are around 17,000 years old.

Mixing paints 6 13
Prehistoric people made their own paints out of natural ingredients such as soil, blood, plant juices, and egg white. From the A.D. 200s, artists began making tempera paint by mixing pigments with egg yolks.

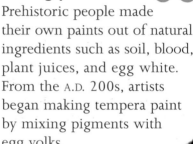
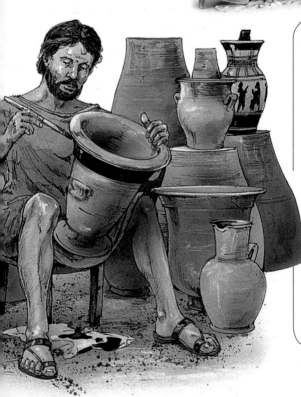

Decorative arts 7

Decorative arts include furniture, pottery, jewelry, metalware, and glassware. Many civilizations have produced beautiful works of decorative art. The ancient Greeks, for example, were famous for their pottery. The pots were often painted in red or black with pictures of Greek heroes.

Oil painting 9 12

In the Renaissance (mid-1300s–1500s), painters crushed up colored minerals and mixed them with oil to make oil paints. Oil paints produce richer colors and dry more slowly than tempera.

Frescoes

A fresco is a painting that is made on the damp plaster of a building. The plaster dries quickly, so the artist has to work fast. Italian artist Michelangelo (1475–1564) painted a famous fresco on the ceiling of the Sistine Chapel in the Vatican in Rome, Italy.

Sculpture

A sculpture is a three-dimensional artistic work. Sculptures are made by carving stone, wood, or other materials. This marble sculpture of Moses was carved by Michelangelo in around 1513.

Van Gogh

The artist Vincent van Gogh (1853–1890) painted *Starry Night* (right) in 1889. He was famous for his expressive use of color.

Pop art

In the 1950s and 1960s pop art became fashionable. On the left is *Blam!* by American artist Roy Lichtenstein (1923–1997).

QUESTIONS:
Ballet

Level 1

1. Do most ballet dancers start as children, teenagers, or adults?
2. Do ballets take place in a rink, a court, or a theater?
3. Do male ballet dancers wear makeup?
4. Is a tutu a ballet shoe, a skirt, or a type of ballet move?

Level 2

5. What type of musician often plays during ballet classes?
6. In *Swan Lake*, what part of the body does a ballerina move to look like wings?
7. Before a show, where do dancers put on their makeup?
8. A port de bras exercise involves the movement of which parts of the body?
9. How many basic positions are there for the feet in ballet?
10. The heels touch together in which position: first, second, or third?
11. ASK LAWNE can be rearranged to give the name of which ballet?
12. Why do dancers wear leg warmers when they practice?
13. What term means "dancing on the tips of the toes"?
14. In a ballet what is the break between acts called?
15. A major ballet may need as many as 30, 300, or 3,000 costumes?

Level 3

16. Which country does the ballet *Swan Lake* come from?
17. What term means the leading female dancer in a ballet company?
18. What "O" is the queen of the swans in *Swan Lake*?

FIND THE ANSWER: Ballet

Ballet is a type of dance that is full of graceful and artistic movements. Ballets are usually set to music and tell a story. Ballet began in Europe in the 1500s and 1600s. Famous ballets include *The Nutcracker* and *The Sleeping Beauty*.

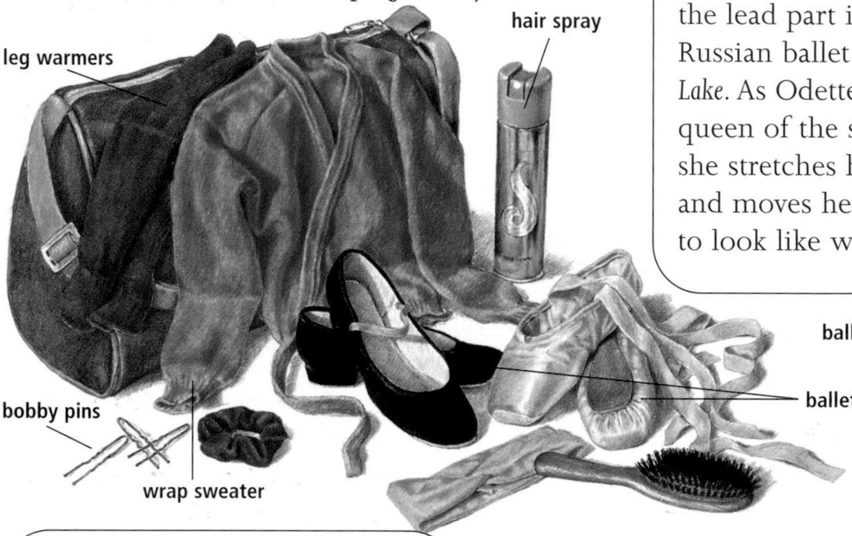

leg warmers

hair spray

bobby pins

wrap sweater

ballet shoes

The ballerina   6 11 16 17 18
"Prima ballerina" means "first dancer" in Italian. It is the name given to the leading female dancer in a ballet company. This dancer is playing the lead part in the Russian ballet *Swan Lake*. As Odette, the queen of the swans, she stretches her neck and moves her arms to look like wings.

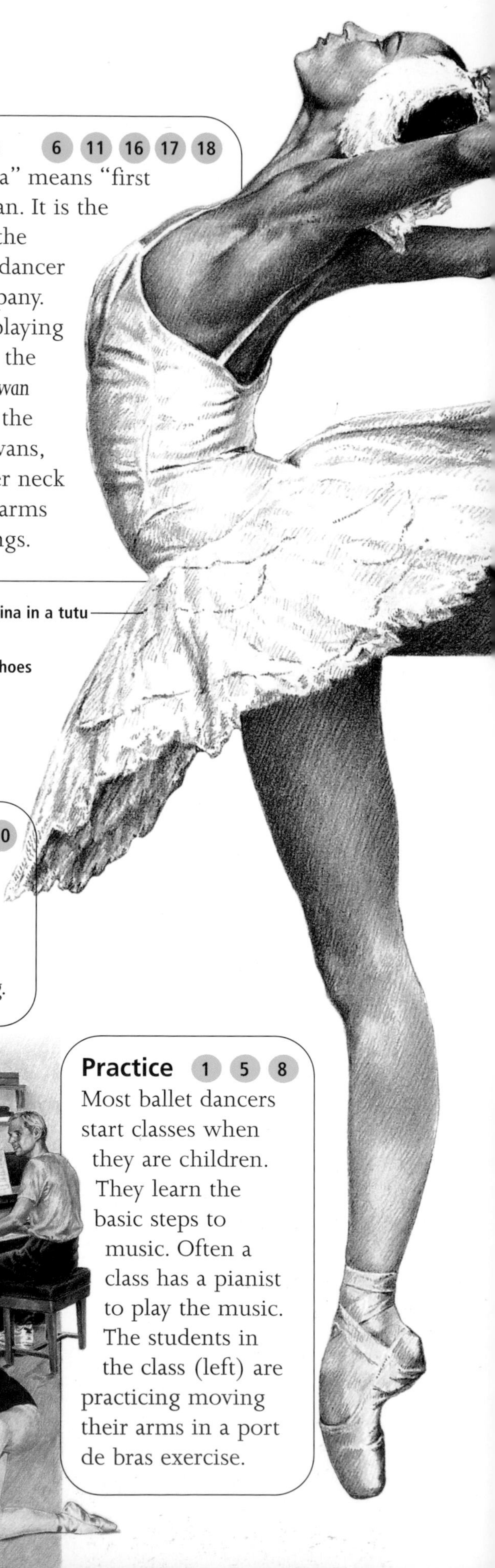

ballerina in a tutu

Clothing   12
Ballet dancers wear special clothes when they practice. Leg warmers and a wrap sweater help keep their muscles warm, preventing strains and injuries.

Positions   9 10
Ballet dancers are taught five basic positions for their feet. In first position, the feet are turned out, with the two heels touching.

Practice   1 5 8
Most ballet dancers start classes when they are children. They learn the basic steps to music. Often a class has a pianist to play the music. The students in the class (left) are practicing moving their arms in a port de bras exercise.

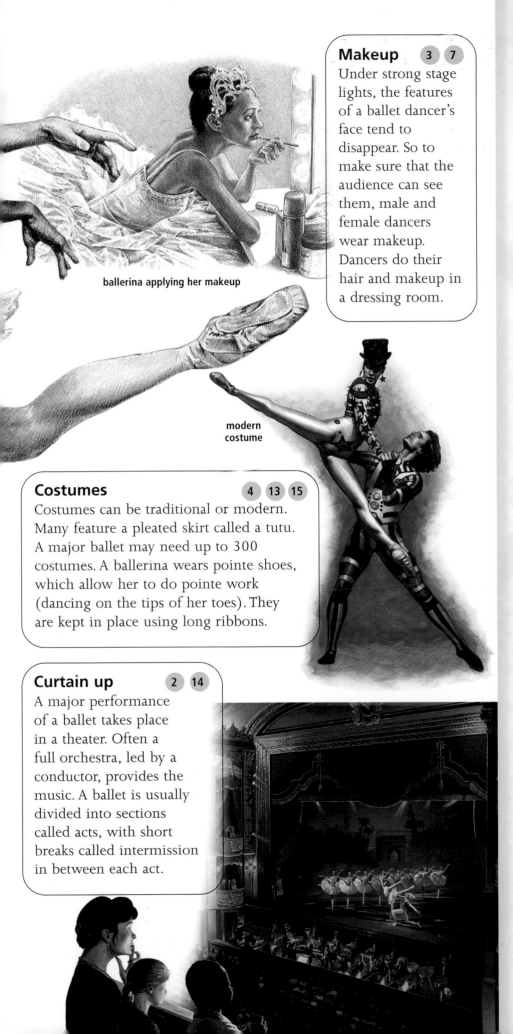

Makeup ③ ⑦

Under strong stage lights, the features of a ballet dancer's face tend to disappear. So to make sure that the audience can see them, male and female dancers wear makeup. Dancers do their hair and makeup in a dressing room.

ballerina applying her makeup

modern costume

Costumes ④ ⑬ ⑮

Costumes can be traditional or modern. Many feature a pleated skirt called a tutu. A major ballet may need up to 300 costumes. A ballerina wears pointe shoes, which allow her to do pointe work (dancing on the tips of her toes). They are kept in place using long ribbons.

Curtain up ② ⑭

A major performance of a ballet takes place in a theater. Often a full orchestra, led by a conductor, provides the music. A ballet is usually divided into sections called acts, with short breaks called intermission in between each act.

QUESTIONS:
Architecture

Level 1

1. Who built the Parthenon: the Greeks, Egyptians, or Romans?
2. What is the name given to the giant buildings used to bury the rulers (pharaohs) in ancient Egypt?
3. Were the first bricks made of mud and clay or cement and gravel?
4. Are the pyramids of ancient Egypt made of mud, wood, or stone?
5. Were the first bricks made solid by setting them on fire, letting them dry in the sun, or freezing them?

Level 2

6. Which civilization invented concrete?
7. Was the Parthenon built of granite, cement, or marble?
8. In which city is the Parthenon?
9. Why does Hardwick Hall have many windows?
10. Did the White House get water pipes or gas lighting installed first?
11. Did the Gothic style of architecture begin in Europe, Asia, or Africa?
12. What is the name of wooden strips that are filled in with daub?
13. Who built Hardwick Hall?

Level 3

14. What are the architect's detailed plans for a building called?
15. Which famous building did James Hoban rebuild?
16. The Parthenon was a temple for the worship of which goddess?
17. What is a flying buttress?
18. During which century did Gothic architecture first appear?

Architecture

Egyptian pyramids

Architecture is the art of designing buildings and structures such as bridges, houses, and temples. Each building has its own purpose, but all architects aim for their buildings to last a long time and to look pleasing. Architects from different civilizations and historical eras have found many different ways of achieving this.

Parthenon 1 7 8 16

The ancient Greeks used stone and marble to build beautiful pillars and structures. An example is the Parthenon in Athens. It was built out of marble in the 5th century B.C. as a temple to the Greek goddess Athena.

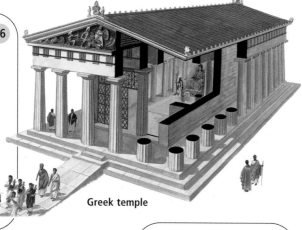

Greek temple

Pyramids 2 4

The ancient Egyptians built enormous burial pyramids for their rulers (pharaohs). The largest of these, the Great Pyramid at Giza, was built more than 4,500 years ago. It is made up of more than two million large stone blocks, each weighing two-and-a-half tons.

Walls 12

In timber-framed buildings wooden strips called wattles formed a frame, filled in with daub— a mixture of straw, mud, and dung.

Building materials 3 5

Over the years people have built with stone, wood, straw, leaves, and grasses. The first bricks were made of mud and clay. These were left to dry and set hard in the sun.

Roman builders 6

The Romans used elements of Greek architecture, like the columns on this house. They were the first to design buildings with arches and even invented concrete, which is still used today.

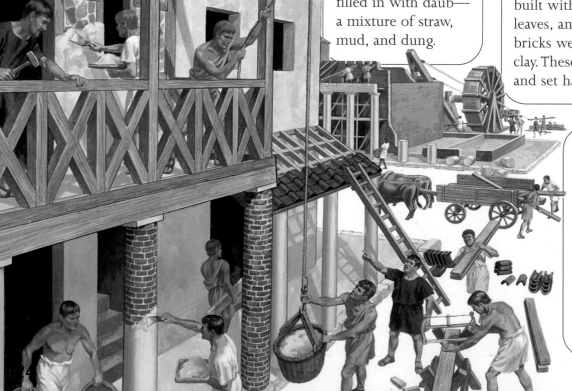

building a house

Churches 11 17 18

A style of architecture called "Gothic" was used for many churches in Europe between 1140 and 1500. A special side support, called a flying buttress, allowed architects to build churches with very thin walls and large windows.

flying buttresses

Stately homes 9 13

A big house showed how rich and powerful a person was. Hardwick Hall in the U.K., built by Bess of Hardwick, has many windows—a sign of wealth in the days when glass was very expensive.

Hardwick Hall

The White House 10 15

The White House in Washington, D.C. was started in 1792. It was burned down in 1814 but was rebuilt by architect James Hoban. Water pipes were installed in 1833, followed by gas lighting (1848), an elevator (1881), and electricity (1891).

Architects' plans 14

Architects produce drawings and plans of their work to discuss with clients (the people who hire them). Modern building plans are called blueprints.

QUESTIONS:
Movies and TV

Level 1

1. Were the first TV broadcasts black-and-white or color?
2. What "D" is the person in charge of the filmmaking process?
3. What name is given to someone who interviews people for the news?
4. What word describes people who play characters and appear in movies?
5. What word describes the written-down version of a movie?

Level 2

6. Who are the three people needed in a news team?
7. What word describes news reporting that is transmitted as the events happen?
8. Was the first movie with sound *Casablanca*, *The Jazz Singer*, or *Snow White*?
9. WOOLY HOLD can be rearranged to give the name of what huge movie industry based in the U.S.?
10. Near which big American city is Hollywood located?
11. What nickname is given to India's movie industry?
12. What name is given to 24-hour news programs?

Level 3

13. Was Telstar the name of an early television or a satellite?
14. In what year was the first "talking" movie made?
15. In 1962 what percentage of U.S. homes had a television?
16. In what year was the first TV signal sent by satellite?
17. What word is used for sending programs out from a TV station?
18. Which Asian country has one of the largest movie industries in the world?

Movies and TV

A movie is made up of a number of photos, called frames, that are shown in a fast sequence to create moving images. Movies are shown using projectors at theaters, or they can be recorded onto videotapes or DVDs. Movies can also be sent (transmitted) through the air or by a cable to people's television sets at home.

Movie crew 8 14

Dozens of people work on the set of a movie. Some help with the costumes, and others build the scenery or operate equipment. When they began, movies had no sound. The first "talking" movie with sound was *The Jazz Singer* in 1927.

Director 2 4 5

The person in charge of making a movie is the director. The director works with the written-down version of the movie (the screenplay) and the people who play the characters in the movie (the actors).

Sets 9 10 11 18

A set is where a movie is shot. It can be inside or outside. Hollywood, near Los Angeles, California, and Mumbai (Bombay), in India, are home to the world's two largest movie industries. India's movie industry is sometimes nicknamed Bollywood.

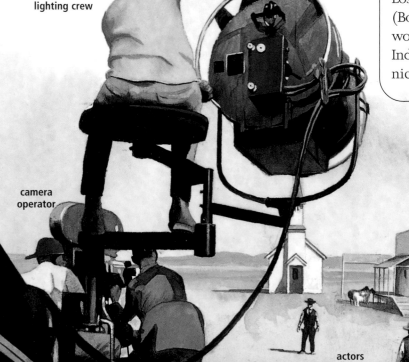

lighting crew

camera operator

actors

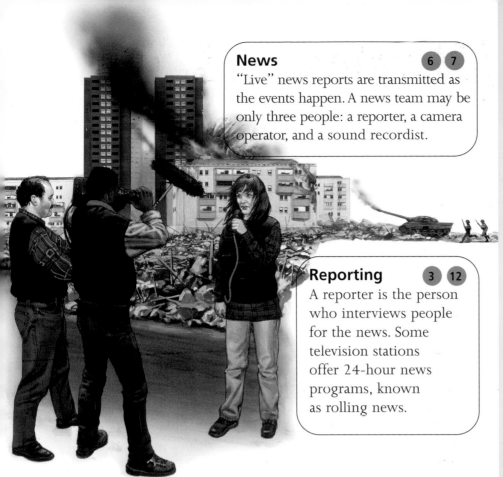

News 6 7
"Live" news reports are transmitted as the events happen. A news team may be only three people: a reporter, a camera operator, and a sound recordist.

Reporting 3 12
A reporter is the person who interviews people for the news. Some television stations offer 24-hour news programs, known as rolling news.

Studio 17
Many TV shows are filmed in a studio. A television camera uses a sensitive electronic tube to change light into electrical signals. These are then sent out to people's homes by transmitters. Sending out a program is known as broadcasting.

Into the home 1 13 15 16
When television began in the 1930s, the programs were in black-and-white. The first color sets were made in the U.S. in 1956. By 1962, 90 percent of U.S. homes had television sets. In the same year the first TV signal was sent by a satellite called Telstar. Today many homes have satellite or cable television.

ANSWERS

Did you get it right? Now that you have finished your *Quiz Quest*, you can turn the page to find the answers. Remember, with the help of a friend, you can also use the answer section for a quick quiz. Why not take turns and see who gets the most right?

ANSWERS:
The rain forest

Level 1
1. Are frogs reptiles or amphibians?
Answer: Amphibians

2. Are reptiles cold-blooded or warm-blooded?
Answer: Cold-blooded

3. The world's longest river begins with "A." What is it?
Answer: The Amazon

4. How often does it usually rain in the rain forest: daily, weekly, or monthly?
Answer: Daily

Level 2
5. In which continent does the cinchona tree grow?
Answer: South America

6. What type of animal is a boa?
Answer: A snake

7. Which plant has the largest flower in the world?
Answer: Rafflesia

8. In which part of the rain forest do most of its animals live?
Answer: The canopy

9. What do pitcher plants feed on?
Answer: Insects

10. What does the flower of the rafflesia plant smell like?
Answer: Rotten meat

11. GREEN STEM can be rearranged to give the name of which group of tall trees?
Answer: Emergents

12. Where in the world do poison dart frogs live?
Answer: South America

13. Is a bromeliad an animal or a plant?
Answer: A plant

14. A poison dart frog's skin has enough poison to kill a person. True or false?
Answer: True

15. Where does the atlas moth live?
Answer: Southeast Asia

Level 3
16. Are snakes more closely related to frogs or lizards?
Answer: Lizards

17. How wide is the Amazon river at its mouth: more than 185 mi. (300km), more than 250 mi. (400km), or more than 300 mi. (500km)?
Answer: More than 185 mi. (300km)

18. What illness is treated with quinine?
Answer: Malaria

19. What part of geckos' bodies gives them a good grip?
Answer: Their toes

20. Where do plants known as epiphytes grow?
Answer: On other plants

ANSWERS:
Ants

Level 1
1. Which have stronger mandibles (jaws): worker or soldier ants?
Answer: Soldier ants

2. What "Q" is the large ant that lays all of the eggs in a colony?
Answer: The queen

3. Are aphids worms or insects?
Answer: They are insects

4. Are wood ants bigger or smaller than most other ants?
Answer: They are bigger

Level 2
5. Are there any ants that bring aphids inside their nests?
Answer: Yes

6. Most ants build nests underground. True or false?
Answer: True

7. What do aphids feed on?
Answer: Plant sap

8. What is the name of the sugary substance that aphids produce?
Answer: Honeydew

9. Are honeypot ants most common in dry or wet places?
Answer: They are most common in dry places

10. Do leaf-cutters live in warm or cold forests?
Answer: They live in warm forests

11. Do wood ants ever bite people?
Answer: Yes

12. What type of substance can some ants fire at attackers?
Answer: Acid

13. What do wood ants build their nests from?
Answer: Pine needles

14. Do ants ever attack birds?
Answer: Yes

Level 3
15. Do leaf-cutters eat the leaves that they harvest?
Answer: No

16. How many different types of ants are there in a colony?
Answer: Three (queen, worker, and soldier ants)

17. What does the word "metamorphose" mean?
Answer: To change shape

18. In what type of forest do most wood ants live?
Answer: Pine forest

19. Do all of the workers in a honeypot ant colony store food inside their bodies?
Answer: No

20. Name a continent in which both honeypot ants and leaf-cutters live.
Answer: North or South America

ANSWERS: Dinosaurs

Level 1

1. What did *Spinosaurus* have on its back: wings or a sail?
   Answer: A sail
2. What "S" was the largest stegosaur?
   Answer: Stegosaurus
3. Which dinosaur had plates on its back: *Kentrosaurus* or *Tyrannosaurus rex*?
   Answer: Kentrosaurus
4. Which had larger teeth: plant-eating or meat-eating dinosaurs?
   Answer: Meat-eating dinosaurs

Level 2

5. *Tyrannosaurus rex* teeth could be almost 4 in. (10cm) long. True or false?
   Answer: True
6. Do fossils take thousands or millions of years to form?
   Answer: Millions of years
7. Did sauropods have long necks or short necks?
   Answer: They had long necks
8. Did any dinosaurs have beaks?
   Answer: Yes
9. What did *Styracosaurus* have on its nose?
   Answer: A horn
10. What did male horned dinosaurs probably use their horns for, besides defense?
    Answer: To fight each other
11. Which are more common: scattered fossil bones or entire fossil skeletons?
    Answer: Scattered fossil bones
12. What type of dinosaur was *Kentrosaurus*?
    Answer: A stegosaur
13. How did a *Spinosaurus* cool down?
    Answer: By pumping blood into its sail
14. Where can you see dinosaur bones on display?
    Answer: At a museum

Level 3

15. What did *Tyrannosaurus rex* eat?
    Answer: Meat
16. Which was bigger: *Seismosaurus* or *Stegosaurus*?
    Answer: Seismosaurus
17. Are fossils made out of bone or of minerals from rocks?
    Answer: Minerals from rocks
18. *Styracosaurus* ate meat. True or false?
    Answer: False
19. Is an *Apatosaurus* more closely related to a *Seismosaurus* or a *Styracosaurus*?
    Answer: Apatosaurus and Seismosaurus are related
20. How many rows of plates did most stegosaurs have?
    Answer: Two

ANSWERS: Snakes

Level 1

1. Are pythons snakes?
   Answer: Yes
2. Do snakes have legs?
   Answer: No
3. Can snakes see?
   Answer: Yes

Level 2

4. Are there any snakes that eat eggs?
   Answer: Yes
5. Which snakes have a hood that they raise when threatened?
   Answer: Cobras
6. Where is a rattlesnake's rattle: in its mouth or on the end of its tail?
   Answer: On the end of its tail
7. Are snakes vertebrates or invertebrates?
   Answer: Vertebrates
8. What are snakes' skeletons made from?
   Answer: Bone
9. Do snakes' eggs have hard or flexible shells?
   Answer: Flexible shells
10. Are there any snakes that give birth to live young?
    Answer: Yes
11. Rattlesnakes live in Africa. True or false?
    Answer: False
12. Do cobras have solid or hollow fangs?
    Answer: Hollow fangs
13. Do anacondas grow to more than 19 in. (50cm) long, more than 9 ft. (3m) long, or more than 26 ft. (8m) long?
    Answer: More than 26 ft. (8m) long
14. Does camouflage make a snake harder or easier to see?
    Answer: Harder to see

Level 3

15. What does a baby snake have on its snout to help it hatch?
    Answer: An egg tooth
16. Why do snakes flick their tongues in and out?
    Answer: To taste the air
17. How do snakes move?
    Answer: By rippling the muscles on the undersides of their bodies
18. How do pythons kill their prey?
    Answer: By constriction (squeezing)
19. What does the African egg-eating snake use to break eggs?
    Answer: Spines sticking down from its backbone

ANSWERS: Sharks

Level 1
1. Are sharks fish or reptiles?
   Answer: Fish
2. The whale shark is the world's biggest fish. True or false?
   Answer: True
3. Do great white sharks eat lions or sea lions?
   Answer: Sea lions
4. Is a shark's egg case called a mermaid's purse or a sailor's purse?
   Answer: A mermaid's purse

Level 2
5. Do sharks have the same set of teeth throughout their lives?
   Answer: No
6. Do basking sharks live in warmer or cooler water than whale sharks?
   Answer: Cooler
7. The biggest great white sharks can grow up to 20 ft. (6m) long. True or false?
   Answer: True
8. What is the name given to the tiny sea creatures that are food for whale sharks?
   Answer: Plankton
9. Which is bigger: the basking shark or the great white shark?
   Answer: The basking shark
10. HE MADE HARM can be rearranged to give the name of which type of shark?
    Answer: Hammerhead
11. How heavy can a whale shark be: 11 tons, 21 tons, or 31 tons?
    Answer: 21 tons
12. Do all sharks lay eggs?
    Answer: No, some give birth to live young
13. The teeth of an individual shark are all the same shape. True or false?
    Answer: True
14. Which shark is more likely to attack people: the great white or the hammerhead?
    Answer: The great white shark
15. Do sharks ever resort to cannibalism (eating each other)?
    Answer: Yes

Level 3
16. What feature of a hammerhead makes it easier to follow a scent trail in the water?
    Answer: Its widely spaced nostrils
17. The second-largest shark in the world is found off the U.S. What is this?
    Answer: The basking shark
18. What is the largest shark to actively hunt prey?
    Answer: The great white shark

ANSWERS: Sea creatures

Level 1
1. How many tentacles does an octopus have?
   Answer: Eight
2. Most of a jellyfish's body is made up of air. True or false?
   Answer: False
3. What does scuba equipment help people do?
   Answer: Breathe underwater
4. Are sea horses fish or mollusks?
   Answer: Fish

Level 2
5. What is the world's largest species of ray?
   Answer: The manta ray
6. Are there more than 100 types of sharks in the world?
   Answer: Yes
7. How many tentacles does a squid have?
   Answer: Ten
8. What do squid eat: jellyfish, plankton, or fish?
   Answer: Fish
9. What do jellyfish use to attack their prey?
   Answer: Stinging tentacles
10. Are squid invertebrates?
    Answer: Yes
11. Which ocean habitat is home to the most types of fish?
    Answer: Coral reefs
12. How long can divers stay underwater for: ten minutes or more, 15 minutes or more, or 20 minutes or more?
    Answer: 20 minutes or more
13. What do the tanks in scuba equipment contain?
    Answer: Compressed gas
14. Are sharks more closely related to squid or rays?
    Answer: Rays
15. Do squid spend most of their time in open water or on the seabed?
    Answer: In open water

Level 3
16. What "P" leaves behind the hard, stony cases that we see in coral reefs?
    Answer: Polyps
17. To which of these creatures are corals most closely related: jellyfish, giant clams, or sharks?
    Answer: Jellyfish
18. What word is used to describe a tail that can grip things?
    Answer: Prehensile

ANSWERS: Marine mammals

Level 1

1. What is the biggest animal on Earth: the elephant or the blue whale?
Answer: The blue whale

2. Do seals eat fish or seaweed?
Answer: Fish

3. By what name are orcas more commonly known: killer whales or seals?
Answer: Killer whales

4. Baby harp seals are born with gray fur. True or false?
Answer: False

Level 2

5. Which use echolocation to find their prey: dolphins or walrus?
Answer: Dolphins

6. What "K" are shrimplike creatures that humpback whales eat?
Answer: Krill

7. Seals give birth in the sea. True or false?
Answer: False

8. Do all walrus have tusks or just males?
Answer: All walrus have tusks

9. What "P" is a group of killer whales known as?
Answer: A pod

10. Why are many large whales rare today?
Answer: Because they were hunted in the past

11. Which marine mammals sometimes kill and eat whales that are larger than they are?
Answer: Killer whales (orcas)

12. Do all whales eat large animals?
Answer: No

13. Which ocean surrounds the North Pole?
Answer: The Arctic Ocean

14. What "S" do walruses eat?
Answer: Shellfish

Level 3

15. Where on a whale would you find its baleen?
Answer: Inside its mouth

16. What "C" is the name of the marine mammal group that contains whales and dolphins?
Answer: Cetaceans

17. Near which pole do walrus live: the North Pole or the South Pole?
Answer: The North Pole

18. What part of a blue whale weighs as much as an elephant?
Answer: Its tongue

19. How long was the largest blue whale ever measured?
Answer: 110 ft. (33.5m) long

ANSWERS: Seabirds

Level 1

1. Do puffins carry food in their mouths, on their feet, or on their wings?
Answer: In their mouths

2. Do seagulls ever feed inland?
Answer: Yes

3. SNIFF UP can be rearranged to give the name of which seabirds?
Answer: Puffins

4. An albatross is a type of seabird. True or false?
Answer: True

5. What "F" is the main food of most seabirds?
Answer: Fish

Level 2

6. Some seabirds carry food for their chicks inside their stomachs. True or false?
Answer: True

7. Why do cormorants stand with their wings open after hunting in the water?
Answer: To dry them off

8. Do puffins use their wings or feet to swim?
Answer: Their wings

9. Do boobies hunt by diving into the water from the air or by diving in from the surface?
Answer: By diving in from the air

10. Is a male frigate bird's throat pouch red, yellow, or blue?
Answer: Red

11. Do cormorants use their wings or feet to swim?
Answer: Their feet

12. Does oil float on water, or does it sink?
Answer: It floats

13. Do frigate birds live in the tropics or near the North Pole?
Answer: In the tropics

Level 3

14. What "G" is a seabird that nests near the tops of cliffs?
Answer: The gannet

15. What does the word "regurgitate" mean?
Answer: To cough up

16. How do frigate birds get food?
Answer: By attacking other birds and stealing their food

17. Why do male frigate birds inflate their throat pouches with air?
Answer: To attract females

18. What "T" is a word for the warm air currents that frigate birds use in order to lift them into the air?
Answer: Thermals

ANSWERS: Birds

Level 1

1. Do birds have teeth?
Answer: No

2. Birds are the only animals in the world that have feathers. True or false?
Answer: True

3. Do birds flap their wings when they are gliding?
Answer: No

4. Can swans fly?
Answer: Yes

Level 2

5. A NEST FILM can be rearranged to give the name of what parts of a feather?
Answer: Filaments

6. What is the world's largest bird?
Answer: The ostrich

7. Birds have elbow joints. True or false?
Answer: True

8. Are birds' bones solid or hollow?
Answer: Hollow

9. GLEAM UP can be rearranged to give what name for the feathers that cover a bird?
Answer: Plumage

10. Does a kestrel eat fruit, seeds, or meat?
Answer: Meat

11. Which are usually more brightly colored: male birds or female birds?
Answer: Male birds

12. Which "H" means to stay still in midair?
Answer: Hover

13. Which has a longer beak: a curlew or a robin?
Answer: A curlew

14. How many times can hummingbirds flap their wings every second: seven times, 70 times, or 700 times?
Answer: 70 times

Level 3

15. What is the chamber between a bird's mouth and its stomach called?
Answer: The crop

16. How many sections does a bird's stomach have?
Answer: Two

17. What do hummingbirds feed on?
Answer: Nectar

18. What "R" is a large, flightless bird?
Answer: Rhea

ANSWERS: African herbivores

Level 1

1. Do zebras have spots or stripes?
Answer: Stripes

2. Are rhinos larger or smaller than rabbits?
Answer: Larger

3. Are zebras more closely related to horses or sheep?
Answer: Horses

4. Where on an elephant's body is its trunk?
Answer: On its face

Level 2

5. What is the world's largest land animal?
Answer: The elephant

6. What is the world's tallest land animal?
Answer: The giraffe

7. What "B" is the word for a male elephant?
Answer: Bull

8. How can an elephant use its trunk to cool itself down?
Answer: By spraying itself with water

9. African elephants can weigh more than one ton. True or false?
Answer: True

10. How tall do male giraffes grow: 10 ft. (3m), 20 ft. (6m), or 30 ft. (10m)?
Answer: 20 ft. (6m)

11. Rhinos have excellent eyesight. True or false?
Answer: False

12. Do giraffes feed mostly on grass, insects, or leaves?
Answer: Leaves

13. Which African predator can kill an elephant?
Answer: The lion

14. How many species (types) of zebras are there: three, five, or seven?
Answer: Three

Level 3

15. What "P" hunts elephants for their tusks?
Answer: Poacher

16. How many species (types) of rhinos are there?
Answer: Five

17. What "J" is a species of rhino that lives in Asia?
Answer: Javan

18. What are elephants' tusks made of?
Answer: Ivory

ANSWERS: Lions

Level 1
1. What is the name for a female lion?
   Answer: Lioness
2. RIP ED can be rearranged to give what name for a group of lions?
   Answer: Pride
3. Which lions have manes: males or females?
   Answer: Males
4. Do male or female lions make up most of a pride?
   Answer: Females
5. Which are bigger: male or female lions?
   Answer: Male lions

Level 2
6. Which are the last members of a pride to feed at a kill?
   Answer: The cubs
7. Besides hunting, what do the lionesses do in the pride?
   Answer: Care for the young
8. Which members of a pride of lions do most of the hunting?
   Answer: The females
9. Do female lions stay with or leave the pride when they grow up?
   Answer: They stay
10. Do lions usually hunt in groups or alone?
    Answer: In groups
11. Do lions ever fight to the death?
    Answer: Yes
12. How long do lion cubs stay hidden from the rest of the pride: eight days, eight weeks, or eight months?
    Answer: Eight weeks
13. What do lion cubs have on their coats that adult lions do not?
    Answer: Spots
14. How many male lions usually lead a pride?
    Answer: One

Level 3
15. What is the name of the area in which a pride of lions lives and hunts?
    Answer: Territory
16. What do lions use to mark the borders of their territory?
    Answer: Urine, droppings, and scratch marks
17. What do male lions do to keep other lions away?
    Answer: They roar
18. How does a male lion take over a pride?
    Answer: He challenges the established male

ANSWERS: Polar animals

Level 1
1. Can penguins fly?
   Answer: No
2. Can polar bears swim?
   Answer: Yes
3. Polar bears can weigh more than one ton. True or false?
   Answer: True
4. Do polar bears ever lie in wait for their prey?
   Answer: Yes
5. Polar bears eat seals. True or false?
   Answer: True

Level 2
6. In which season do migrating birds arrive in the polar regions?
   Answer: The spring
7. Killer whales live in polar waters. True or false?
   Answer: True
8. Why do some types of baby seals have white coats?
   Answer: To hide them in the snow
9. Do polar bears live close to the North Pole or the South Pole?
   Answer: The North Pole
10. Penguins live in the Antarctic. True or false?
    Answer: True
11. ALE BUG can be rearranged to give the name of which whale that lives in the Arctic waters?
    Answer: Beluga
12. Which sense do polar bears use to find most of their prey: sight, hearing, or smell?
    Answer: Smell
13. How do penguins paddle through the water: with their wings or with their feet?
    Answer: With their wings
14. What is the world's largest type of penguin?
    Answer: The emperor penguin

Level 3
15. Which bird flies all the way from the Antarctic to the Arctic and back again every year?
    Answer: The Arctic tern
16. How can people protect baby seals from humans who hunt them for their fur?
    Answer: By spraying the seals with a harmless dye
17. Do narwhals live close to the North Pole or the South Pole?
    Answer: Close to the North Pole
18. What word is used for keeping an egg warm until it hatches?
    Answer: Incubating

ANSWERS: Farm animals

Level 1
1. Are dairy cows raised for their milk or their fur?
   Answer: Their milk
2. Is a rooster a male or a female chicken?
   Answer: Male
3. What animal do farmers raise to hunt rats and mice?
   Answer: A cat
4. Which farm animals produce wool?
   Answer: Sheep

Level 2
5. What "K" is a baby goat?
   Answer: Kid
6. Today dairy cows are milked by hand. True or false?
   Answer: False
7. On which part of a cow are its teats?
   Answer: On its udder
8. How many teats does a cow have?
   Answer: Four
9. Which have larger crests on their heads: male or female chickens?
   Answer: Male chickens
10. Which animal is needed to make butter?
    Answer: A cow
11. EAGER FERN can be rearranged to give the name of what type of chicken?
    Answer: Free-range
12. Which farm animal does pork come from?
    Answer: Pigs
13. What "L" is a meat from sheep?
    Answer: Lamb
14. What "F" is removed from a sheep by shearing it?
    Answer: Fleece

Level 3
15. What is the smallest piglet in a litter called?
    Answer: A runt
16. How many teats does a goat have?
    Answer: Two
17. What type of dog is a border collie?
    Answer: A sheepdog
18. What is a male pig called?
    Answer: A boar
19. What is the name for chickens that are kept in cages?
    Answer: Battery chickens

SANSWERS: Horses

Level 1
1. What are baby horses called?
   Answer: Foals
2. What do cowboys wear to shade them from the sun?
   Answer: Wide-brimmed hats
3. In show jumping, do riders try to jump over obstacles or crash into them?
   Answer: They try to jump over obstacles
4. Horses are used to pull plows. True or false?
   Answer: True
5. What "L" is the looped rope that cowboys use to catch cattle?
   Answer: Lasso
6. Are ponies larger or smaller than horses?
   Answer: Smaller

Level 2
7. Is an Exmoor a breed of pony or a breed of horse?
   Answer: A breed of pony
8. What is the largest breed of horse?
   Answer: The Shire horse
9. What is the main difference between the skeleton of a horse and the skeleton of a human?
   Answer: Horse skeletons have front legs instead of arms
10. When do male horses show their teeth and pull back their lips?
    Answer: When they smell a female horse
11. HEN CARS can be rearranged to give the name of what large farms where cowboys work?
    Answer: Ranches
12. What is worn by jumping horses to protect their ankles from knocks?
    Answer: Bandages
13. BANDY HURDS can be rearranged to give the name of what item used for removing dirt from a horse's coat?
    Answer: Dandy brush

Level 3
14. What "C" is a type of pony from Iran?
    Answer: A Caspian pony
15. How does a horse show aggression?
    Answer: By holding back its ears
16. What is the name of the bones that make up a horse's spine?
    Answer: Vertebrae
17. What type of brush is used to brush away loose hair on a horse?
    Answer: A currycomb
18. What "D" is a horse-riding sport that tests obedience and rider control?
    Answer: Dressage

ANSWERS: Cats

Level 1

1. What are baby cats called?
   Answer: Kittens
2. Is catnip a type of plant or a type of animal?
   Answer: A type of plant
3. Do cats creep up and pounce on their prey or chase it around and around until it is exhausted?
   Answer: They creep up and pounce
4. Do cat owners use brushes for grooming their cats or for feeding them?
   Answer: For grooming them
5. Can cats climb?
   Answer: Yes
6. Do young cats prefer playing with balls of string or with knitting needles?
   Answer: With balls of string
7. Are cats good at jumping?
   Answer: Yes

Level 2

8. Cats have claws. True or false?
   Answer: True
9. What is a scratching post for?
   Answer: Keeping a cat's claws sharp
10. Do cats prefer to live alone or in groups?
    Answer: Alone
11. For how long do a cat's eyes stay closed after it is born?
    Answer: One week
12. How often should cats be fed?
    Answer: At least once each day
13. Which fight more often: male cats or female cats?
    Answer: Male cats
14. What are male cats called?
    Answer: Tomcats
15. Why is it a good idea to use a special dish to feed a cat?
    Answer: So that they come running when their owner approaches it

Level 3

16. What part of a cat's body can be retracted (pulled back)?
    Answer: Its claws
17. From which animal are domestic cats descended?
    Answer: The African wildcat
18. Why do cats spray and mark things with their scent?
    Answer: To warn other cats to stay away from their territory

ANSWERS: Dogs

Level 1

1. What is a baby dog called?
   Answer: A puppy
2. Are most police dogs Alsatians or Dalmatians?
   Answer: Alsatians
3. Were pit bulls originally bred for fighting or bringing slippers?
   Answer: For fighting
4. Are most Labradors friendly or aggressive?
   Answer: Friendly
5. The terrier is the largest breed of dog. True or false?
   Answer: False

Level 2

6. What is a group of related puppies called?
   Answer: A litter
7. How long does it take for a puppy to grow into an adult: six months, one year, or three years?
   Answer: One year
8. Which "S" is a type of dog that is often trained to be a sniffer dog?
   Answer: A spaniel
9. How might a hearing dog help a deaf owner?
   Answer: By alerting them if there is a knock on the door
10. If a dog wags its tail, is it happy or angry?
    Answer: Happy
11. Does a sad dog drop its tail or raise it?
    Answer: It drops it
12. Which wild animal is the ancestor of all domestic dogs?
    Answer: The wolf
13. EDGIER REVEL TORN can be rearranged to spell what breed of dog, often trained as a guide dog?
    Answer: Golden retriever
14. Which would make a better guard dog: a Rottweiler or a Labrador?
    Answer: A Rottweiler

Level 3

15. How long should you wait before giving away puppies to new owners?
    Answer: A few weeks
16. During which year of a dog's life is it easiest to train?
    Answer: Its first year
17. What is another word for cutting off a dog's tail?
    Answer: Docking
18. How can you tell when a dog is frightened?
    Answer: It holds its tail between its legs
19. What type of dog was bred to hunt large animals?
    Answer: Hound

ANSWERS: Continents

Level 1

1. Where is the Nile river?
    Answer: In Africa
2. Which continent lies to the east of Europe?
    Answer: Asia
3. Is Asia the second-most-populated continent?
    Answer: No (it is the most populated)
4. Is Central America part of North America or South America?
    Answer: North America
5. What is the smallest continent?
    Answer: Australasia

Level 2

6. What is the world's largest country?
    Answer: The Russian Federation
7. What divides Europe from Africa?
    Answer: The Mediterranean Sea
8. What population milestone was reached in 1802?
    Answer: The world's population reached one billion
9. Is Sydney the capital of Australia?
    Answer: No (Canberra is the capital)
10. In which continent would you find the world's highest mountains?
    Answer: Asia
11. What larger landmass encompasses Europe?
    Answer: Eurasia
12. How many billion people did the world's population reach in 1999: one, five, six, or 11?
    Answer: Six
13. Are the Andes mountains on the east or west coast of South America?
    Answer: On the west coast

Level 3

14. How much of the Amazon rain forest lies outside of Brazil?
    Answer: 40 percent
15. What are the names of the island groups of Australasia?
    Answer: Melanesia, Micronesia, and Polynesia
16. By how many million people per year was the world's population increasing in 2004?
    Answer: 75 million per year
17. How many countries are in Africa: 47, 52, or 53?
    Answer: 53
18. In which continent is the world's largest freshwater lake?
    Answer: In North America
19. How long is the Andes mountain range?
    Answer: 4,340 mi. (7,000km) long

ANSWERS: International community

Level 1

1. The United Nations was formed during World War I. True or false?
    Answer: False
2. What does NATO stand for: the North Atlantic Treaty Organization or the North Antarctic Treaty Organization?
    Answer: The North Atlantic Treaty Organization
3. All peacekeeping units are armed. True or false?
    Answer: False
4. What is the single currency of the European Union?
    Answer: The euro
5. CRESS ROD can be rearranged to give the name of what organization that provides medical aid?
    Answer: The Red Cross

Level 2

6. Why was NATO formed?
    Answer: To ensure peace in its member states
7. What convention protects wounded soldiers and prisoners?
    Answer: The Geneva Convention
8. In what city is the UN headquarters?
    Answer: New York City
9. How many countries are in the UN?
    Answer: 191
10. What treaty marked the beginning of the European Union?
    Answer: The Treaty of Paris
11. In what building do member nations of the UN meet?
    Answer: The General Assembly building
12. For what purpose can peacekeeping units use their weapons?
    Answer: For self-defense

Level 3

13. In what year did the UN headquarters officially open?
    Answer: 1951
14. What treaty led to the formation of the European Union?
    Answer: The Maastricht Treaty
15. What is the full name of the Red Cross?
    Answer: The International Committee of the Red Cross and the Red Crescent Movement
16. How much money was donated to buy land for the UN headquarters?
    Answer: $8.5 million
17. What is the name of the central command of NATO's military forces?
    Answer: SHAPE (Supreme Headquarters Allied Powers Europe)
18. Who first used the term "United Nations"?
    Answer: U.S. President Franklin D. Roosevelt

ANSWERS: Flags

Level 1

1. What colors could a pirate flag be?
Answer: Red or black

2. Where are navy flags used: at sea or in space?
Answer: At sea

3. In what type of sport is a black-and-white checkered flag used?
Answer: In car and motorcycle racing

4. What type of flag do explorers place on lands that they have discovered?
Answer: Their national flag

5. Which has the oldest national flag: Scotland or the United States?
Answer: Scotland

Level 2

6. Which sport uses flags: football, cycling, or rowing?
Answer: All three

7. What are navy flags called?
Answer: Signaling flags

8. What event prompted the French flag to be redesigned?
Answer: The French Revolution

9. Are signaling flags used alone or together?
Answer: Both alone and together

10. What is semaphore?
Answer: A signaling system using flags

11. How many U.S. flags have been placed on the Moon: four, five, or six?
Answer: Six

12. Which color is not used in navy flags: yellow, black, or green?
Answer: Green

Level 3

13. What do referees use flags to indicate in a football game?
Answer: A penalty

14. In semaphore, how is an "R" signaled?
Answer: By holding both arms and flags straight out

15. On a pirate flag, what does an hourglass symbolize?
Answer: That time is running out

16. What color flags are used in semaphore?
Answer: Red and yellow

17. In which century were pirate flags first used?
Answer: The 18th century

18. What displayed a U.S. flag on Mars?
Answer: The Viking lander

ANSWERS: Natural wonders

Level 1

1. What is the tallest mountain in the world?
Answer: Mount Everest

2. What is the tallest waterfall in the world?
Answer: Angel Falls

3. K2 is in Europe. True or false?
Answer: False

4. The Great Barrier Reef lies off the coast of which country?
Answer: Australia

5. The Great Barrier Reef can be seen from space. True or false?
Answer: True

6. Which is longer: the Grand Canyon or the Great Barrier Reef?
Answer: The Great Barrier Reef

Level 2

7. Who were the first people to reach the top of Mount Everest?
Answer: Edmund Hillary and Tenzing Norgay

8. How is the length of the Grand Canyon measured?
Answer: By the Colorado river

9. How many times higher is Angel Falls than Niagara Falls: ten, 15, or 20?
Answer: 15 times

10. What is the Hillary Step?
Answer: A steep section of Mount Everest

11. How old are the rocks in the Grand Canyon?
Answer: Two billion years old

12. In what continent is the widest waterfall in the world?
Answer: Asia

13. What is another name for *aurora borealis*?
Answer: The northern lights

Level 3

14. What causes the northern lights?
Answer: High-speed particles from the Sun colliding with gas molecules

15. How much older are the Alps than the Himalayas?
Answer: 15 million years

16. How high is Mount Everest?
Answer: 29,000 ft. (8,850m) high

17. What is the Latin name of the southern lights?
Answer: Aurora australis

18. What geographical feature is 35,368 ft. (10,783m) wide?
Answer: Khone Falls

ANSWERS:
Coasts

Level 1
1. A tsunami is caused by the wind. True or false?
Answer: False
2. ACE VASE can be rearranged to give what name for a cavern in a cliff?
Answer: Sea cave
3. What is the wearing down of a headland called: erosion or erasure?
Answer: Erosion
4. What two materials do waves deposit on beaches?
Answer: Pebbles and sand
5. What "W" causes waves?
Answer: The wind
6. HELLO BOW can be rearranged to give the name of what coastal feature?
Answer: Blowhole

Level 2
7. What is special about the Painted Cave?
Answer: It is the longest sea cave in the world
8. What does the word "tsunami" mean?
Answer: Harbor wave
9. What causes water to gush through a blowhole?
Answer: Built-up air pressure
10. The fetch is the material deposited on a beach. True or false?
Answer: False
11. A stack is a mound of sand. True or false?
Answer: False
12. Is seawater acidic or alkaline?
Answer: Acidic

Level 3
13. Which is formed first: a cave or a blowhole?
Answer: A cave
14. How fast do tsunami waves move?
Answer: At more than 430 mph (700km/h)
15. What coastal process do groins prevent?
Answer: Longshore drift
16. On what island is the Painted Cave?
Answer: Santa Cruz island, California
17. How high can tsunamis be?
Answer: Up to 98 ft. (30m) high
18. A stack is formed from which coastal feature?
Answer: An arch

ANSWERS:
Rivers

Level 1
1. What is the beginning of a river called?
Answer: The source
2. In what continent are the Great Lakes?
Answer: North America
3. Do waterfalls flow over a ledge of hard or soft rock?
Answer: Hard rock
4. What is the name of the process by which water moves between the land and sea and back again?
Answer: The water cycle
5. What is the name of the area of flat land on both sides of a river?
Answer: A floodplain

Level 2
6. What "R" is precipitation?
Answer: Rain
7. What type of lakes are created by ice sheets?
Answer: Freshwater lakes
8. What is formed when a river floods shallow lakes or ponds?
Answer: A marsh
9. Do tributaries increase or decrease the water volume of a river?
Answer: Increase
10. What happens to evaporated water?
Answer: It condenses to form clouds
11. What other name is used for an estuary?
Answer: A harbor
12. Headwaters are the top of a waterfall. True or false?
Answer: False
13. What prevents water seepage in a marshland?
Answer: Granite, slate, or quartz beneath
14. What forms at the bottom of a waterfall?
Answer: A plunge pool

Level 3
15. What "Y" is a waterfall in the U.S., created by a glacier?
Answer: Yosemite Falls in California
16. What name is given to fertile land formed on a floodplain?
Answer: Alluvium
17. What can form from sediment in an estuary?
Answer: A delta
18. How was Lake Tanganyika formed?
Answer: By Earth fault movements

ANSWERS: Deserts

Level 1

1. What "D" is a sandy desert feature?
   Answer: Dune
2. Which animal is used to carry people and goods in the desert?
   Answer: The camel
3. Sand holds water. True or false?
   Answer: False
4. What plant with spines can survive in a desert?
   Answer: The cactus
5. What "B" is the home of a meerkat?
   Answer: A burrow

Level 2

6. Is a Tuareg a type of sand dune or a member of a desert tribe?
   Answer: A member of a desert tribe
7. What type of sand dune forms when the wind blows in all directions?
   Answer: A star dune
8. What is a one-humped camel called?
   Answer: A dromedary
9. What is the name for wind carrying away fine sand?
   Answer: Deflation
10. What is the slope of a sand dune called?
    Answer: A slip face
11. Wind blowing in two different directions creates which type of sand dune?
    Answer: A linear dune
12. Is a hoodoo: a type of sand dune, a rock formation, or a desert rodent?
    Answer: A rock formation
13. In which desert would you find a Tuareg?
    Answer: The Sahara desert

Level 3

14. What desert plant can be more than 200 years old?
    Answer: The Saguaro cactus
15. What "F" is a type of fox that lives in the desert?
    Answer: The fennec fox
16. What is a barchan?
    Answer: A curved sand dune
17. What substance is formed by cemented sand and gravel?
    Answer: Calcrete
18. What features of a camel help it survive in deserts?
    Answer: It can go without water for several days and has thick padded feet so that it can walk across hot sand without feeling any pain

ANSWERS: The poles

Level 1

1. On which continent is the South Pole?
   Answer: Antarctica
2. The explorer Robert Scott reached the South Pole. True or false?
   Answer: True
3. LIE CRAG can be rearranged to give the name of what polar feature?
   Answer: Glacier
4. Icebergs are lumps of ice that have broken away from glaciers. True or false?
   Answer: True

Level 2

5. What is a hollow formed by melting blocks of ice called: a kettle hole or a sinkhole?
   Answer: A kettle hole
6. How much of an iceberg is visible above the waterline?
   Answer: One tenth
7. Who was the first person to reach the South Pole?
   Answer: Roald Amundsen
8. Why do glaciers shift?
   Answer: Because of the weight of ice and gravity
9. Today most Inuit use dogsleds to travel over the Arctic ice. True or false?
   Answer: False
10. What imaginary line runs between the two poles?
    Answer: The axis on which Earth spins
11. What is a moraine?
    Answer: A ridge of rock left by a melting glacier
12. What language is spoken by the Inuit?
    Answer: Inuktitut
13. What "P" is an item of clothing worn by Arctic people?
    Answer: A parka

Level 3

14. Do the Inuit live close to the North Pole or the South Pole?
    Answer: The North Pole
15. In which year did a person reach the South Pole for the first time?
    Answer: 1911
16. Near which pole are flat-topped tabular icebergs found?
    Answer: The South Pole
17. How far would Robert Scott and his crew have had to travel to safety on the South Pole?
    Answer: 10.5 mi. (17km)
18. What Arctic people live in Greenland?
    Answer: The Kalaalit

Level 1

1. The first living creature in space was a mouse. True or false?
Answer: False

2. Who was the first person on the Moon: Neil Armstrong, Nelly Armstrong, or Norman Armstrong?
Answer: Neil Armstrong

3. ENVISION OUT can be rearranged to give the name of what group of republics?
Answer: The Soviet Union

4. What "S" is an object that orbits Earth?
Answer: Satellite

Level 2

5. What "L" was the name of the first living creature in space?
Answer: Laika

6. What "S" was the first artificial satellite?
Answer: Sputnik

7. AN AIR RIG GUY can be rearranged to give the name of what astronaut, the first person to go into space?
Answer: Yuri Gagarin

8. In which year did people first walk on the Moon: 1959, 1969, or 1979?
Answer: 1969

9. In which year did a person first go into space: 1941, 1951, or 1961?
Answer: 1961

10. Who said, "That's one small step for man, one giant leap for mankind"?
Answer: Neil Armstrong

11. VAN OR RULER can be rearranged to give the name of what vehicle used on the surface of the Moon?
Answer: Lunar rover

12. For how long did the first person who went into space stay there: 89 minutes, 89 hours, or 89 days?
Answer: 89 minutes

Level 3

13. Which was the last *Apollo* mission to land people on the Moon?
Answer: Apollo 17

14. In what year did *Apollo 17* reach the Moon?
Answer: 1972

15. What are Soviet astronauts called?
Answer: Cosmonauts

16. What "V" was the first manned spacecraft?
Answer: Vostock 1

17. What was launched on April 12, 1981?
Answer: The first space shuttle

18. Where is the Baikonur Cosmodrome: in Kazakhstan, Ukraine, or the Russian Federation?
Answer: Kazakhstan

Level 1

1. Which planet do people live on?
Answer: Earth

2. How many planets are in the solar system: seven, nine, or 11?
Answer: Nine

3. MY CURER can be rearranged to give the name of which planet?
Answer: Mercury

Level 2

4. On the part of a planet facing away from the Sun, is it nighttime or daytime?
Answer: Nighttime

5. How many planets in our solar system have names that begin with the letter "M"?
Answer: Two (Mars and Mercury)

6. Which planet is the farthest from the Sun?
Answer: Pluto

7. A GANG SITS can be rearranged to give the name of what group of large planets?
Answer: Gas giants

8. What is the smallest planet in the solar system?
Answer: Pluto

9. The Sun is a star. True or false?
Answer: True

10. Are there any planets in the solar system that are bigger than the Sun?
Answer: No

11. Did the planets form at around the same time as the Sun or long before?
Answer: Around the same time

12. Which "S" is a planet made mostly of hydrogen and helium?
Answer: Saturn

13. How long does Earth take to circle the Sun: one day, one month, or one year?
Answer: One year

14. What "O" is the path that planets take around the Sun?
Answer: Orbit

15. Which takes longer to circle the Sun: Earth or Pluto?
Answer: Pluto

16. How many planets in the solar system have oceans of water?
Answer: One

Level 3

17. What "N" is a swirling cloud of particles from which planets form?
Answer: Nebula

18. Which is farther from the Sun: Uranus or Saturn?
Answer: Uranus

19. Which is larger: Earth or Mars?
Answer: Earth

ANSWERS:
Volcanoes and earthquakes

Level 1
1. Is the surface of Earth made of solid or liquid rock?
   Answer: Solid rock
2. What is another name for Earth's surface: the skin, crust, or coat?
   Answer: The crust
3. RUIN POET can be rearranged to give what word for a volcano exploding?
   Answer: Eruption
4. A seismologist is a type of earthquake. True or false?
   Answer: False (a seismologist is a scientist who studies earthquakes)

Level 2
5. What "R" is the scale used to measure the strength of earthquakes?
   Answer: Richter
6. Which are thicker: continental plates or oceanic plates?
   Answer: Continental plates
7. Are most earthquakes strong enough to destroy buildings?
   Answer: No
8. How thick is Earth's mantle: 180 mi. (290km) or 1,800 mi. (2,900km)?
   Answer: 1,800 mi. (2,900km)
9. Do ridges form where plates move together or where they move apart?
   Answer: Where they move apart
10. Earthquakes are common where plates slide past one another. True or false?
    Answer: True
11. Japan is situated where two plates meet. True or false?
    Answer: True
12. What "L" is the molten rock released by a volcanic eruption?
    Answer: Lava
13. What "F" is the force produced by plates sliding past each other?
    Answer: Friction
14. CUBOID NUTS can be rearranged to give the name of what plate movement?
    Answer: Subduction
15. Volcanoes may occur where two plates are moving apart. True or false?
    Answer: True

Level 3
16. What is the most common substance in Earth's core?
    Answer: Iron
17. Which makes up a greater proportion of Earth: the crust or mantle?
    Answer: The mantle
18. On which plate do volcanoes occur when an oceanic plate and a continental plate meet?
    Answer: On the continental plate

ANSWERS:
Rocks and minerals

Level 1
1. Emeralds are purple. True or false?
   Answer: False
2. What color are rubies?
   Answer: Red
3. Gold is a metal. True or false?
   Answer: True
4. How many sides does a hexagon have: one, three, or six?
   Answer: Six

Level 2
5. TEARING can be rearranged to give the name of what igneous rock, often used for building?
   Answer: Granite
6. Crystals form underground. True or false?
   Answer: True
7. Do sedimentary rocks form on the bottoms of seas, lakes, and rivers or deep within Earth?
   Answer: On the bottoms of seas, lakes, and rivers
8. What word is used for rocks that form under great pressure or heat: metamorphic, mathematic, or metaphysical?
   Answer: Metamorphic
9. Is basalt an igneous or a sedimentary rock?
   Answer: Igneous
10. Gems are cut and polished to make gemstones. True or false?
    Answer: False (gemstones are cut and polished to make gems)
11. What "C" is the substance from which diamonds are formed?
    Answer: Carbon
12. Which are the most valuable: diamonds, emeralds, or garnets?
    Answer: Diamonds
13. HIS PAPER can be rearranged to give the name of what valuable gemstone?
    Answer: Sapphire
14. A START can be rearranged to give what word for layers of rocks?
    Answer: Strata

Level 3
15. In which country is the Giant's Causeway?
    Answer: Northern Ireland
16. What "M" is molten rock, which cools to form igneous rock?
    Answer: Magma
17. What is the name for a stone that has had its edges worn smooth by the action of water?
    Answer: A pebble
18. What "E" cannot be broken down into any simpler substance?
    Answer: An element

ANSWERS: Weather

Level 1

1. Does weather happen in the atmosphere or under the sea?
Answer: In the atmosphere

2. Are clouds made of cotton balls or water vapor?
Answer: Water vapor

3. What "O" is the gas we must breathe in order to stay alive?
Answer: Oxygen

4. What "L" is the word for an electrical charge released from a storm cloud?
Answer: Lightning

5. A weather balloon is a type of cloud. True or false?
Answer: False

Level 2

6. Where does the majority of the water vapor in clouds originally come from?
Answer: The sea

7. Does a weather vane measure wind speed or wind direction?
Answer: Wind direction

8. Which is usually associated with good weather: high pressure or low pressure?
Answer: High pressure

9. What "R" is sometimes formed as sunlight passes through raindrops?
Answer: A rainbow

10. Do rainbows appear when it rains or when there is no rain?
Answer: When it rains

11. Do raindrops become bigger or smaller as they fall through a cloud?
Answer: Bigger

12. What "H" is a word for frozen raindrops?
Answer: Hail

13. Do clouds become cooler or hotter as they rise?
Answer: Cooler

14. REACH RUIN can be rearranged to give the name of what powerful storm?
Answer: Hurricane

15. RING TONE can be rearranged to give the name of which very common gas?
Answer: Nitrogen

Level 3

16. What is a scientist who studies the weather called?
Answer: A meteorologist

17. How many colors are there in a rainbow?
Answer: Seven

18. What "S" do weather forecasters use to watch storms building up in the atmosphere?
Answer: Satellites

ANSWERS: Bones and muscles

Level 1

1. BELOW can be rearranged to give the name of what joint in the middle of the arm?
Answer: Elbow

2. Are there muscles in the human leg?
Answer: Yes

3. What "S" is the name for all the bones in the body put together?
Answer: Skeleton

Level 2

4. Do people have joints in their fingers?
Answer: Yes

5. Muscles contain millions of cells called fibers. True or false?
Answer: True

6. What "B" is a muscle in the arm that helps raise the forearm?
Answer: The biceps

7. Which bones form a cage that protect the internal organs?
Answer: The ribs

8. What "C" is the correct name for the gristle in human bodies?
Answer: Cartilage

9. Which bone links the legs to the backbone?
Answer: The pelvis

10. The patella is another name for which bone?
Answer: The kneecap

11. The muscles in the heart work automatically. True or false?
Answer: True

12. When a person raises their forearm, do their triceps contract or relax?
Answer: Relax

13. How many bones are there in an adult's skull: two, 12, or 22?
Answer: 22

14. Do people have more muscles or more bones in their bodies?
Answer: More muscles

15. Is the shoulder joint a hinge joint or a ball-and-socket joint?
Answer: A ball-and-socket joint

16. What is the largest bone in the human body?
Answer: The thighbone (femur)

17. What is the name of the eight bones that, together, encase the brain?
Answer: The cranium

Level 3

18. The mandible is another name for which part of the body?
Answer: The lower jaw

19. In which part of the body is the smallest bone?
Answer: The ear

20. How many bones are there in the human skeleton?
Answer: 206

ANSWERS: Medicine

Level 1

1. What "D" is the person people visit when they are feeling sick?
Answer: Doctor

2. What vehicles take people to the hospital: ambulances, fire engines, or tractors?
Answer: Ambulances

3. Are ambulances part of the emergency services?
Answer: Yes

4. Do nurses work in hospitals or stores?
Answer: In hospitals

Level 2

5. Broken bones heal themselves. True or false?
Answer: True

6. What "S" is used to listen to a person's heartbeat?
Answer: Stethoscope

7. What does a thermometer measure?
Answer: Body temperature

8. Is intensive care given to people who are very sick or to people who are better, just before they leave the hospital?
Answer: People who are very sick

9. What "S" is the word for a person who carries out operations?
Answer: Surgeon

10. What "T" means to replace a damaged body part with a new, healthy one?
Answer: Transplant

11. Would you wear a cast if you had the flu or if you had a broken leg?
Answer: If you had a broken leg

12. A SCARED IMP can be rearranged to give the name of what people who care for patients on the way to the hospital?
Answer: Paramedics

13. A symptom is a type of medicine. True or false?
Answer: False

14. What "S" is a large machine that looks inside people's bodies?
Answer: Scanner

Level 3

15. What "D" means "to figure out what is wrong with a patient"?
Answer: Diagnose

16. What type of injury can be treated by traction?
Answer: A broken bone

17. What is used to transfer nutrients straight into a person's bloodstream?
Answer: An IV

18. What "M" is a type of wave that scanners use to look inside a body?
Answer: Magnetic

ANSWERS: Trains

Level 1

1. Which came first: steam engines or electric trains?
Answer: Steam engines

2. Do all trains carry passengers?
Answer: No

3. Is diesel a type of fuel or a type of food?
Answer: A type of fuel

4. Who built the train that ran on the first-ever steam railroad: Richard Trevithick, Richard Gere, or Richard the Lionheart?
Answer: Richard Trevithick

5. What "C" was burned in steam engines?
Answer: Coal

Level 2

6. Was the Wild West in Europe or in the United States?
Answer: In the U.S.

7. Is steam created by heating water or by heating gasoline?
Answer: Heating water

8. Which country has bullet trains and super expresses?
Answer: Japan

9. What "R" was a famous steam engine built by George Stephenson?
Answer: The Rocket

10. Which country has TGVs?
Answer: France

11. Are there any trains that can go faster than 125 mph (200km/h)?
Answer: Yes (Japanese bullet trains regularly run at more than 185 mph/300km/h)

12. What "C" on Wild West trains was used for moving cattle off the line?
Answer: Cowcatchers

13. Were steam trains cleaner or dirtier than modern trains?
Answer: Dirtier

Level 3

14. In which country was the world's first-ever steam railroad?
Answer: Wales

15. In which century was the first railroad to cross North America built?
Answer: The 19th century

16. What "F" is the word used for the goods carried by some trains?
Answer: Freight

17. How long was the world's longest-ever train: 3 mi. (5km), 4 mi. (6km), or 5 mi. (7km)?
Answer: 4 mi. (6km)

18. What "P" were exploring settlers who traveled into the Wild West by train?
Answer: Pioneers

ANSWERS: Early flight

Level 1

1. GIRDLE can be rearranged to give the name of what type of unpowered aircraft?
Answer: Glider

2. The first manned flight was in a hot-air balloon. True or false?
Answer: True

3. Is a dirigible a steerable airship or an Australian musical instrument?
Answer: A steerable airship

Level 2

4. What "H" is a type of aircraft with rotating blades?
Answer: Helicopter

5. Which body of water was Louis Blériot the first to fly across in 1909: the English Channel or the Atlantic Ocean?
Answer: The English Channel

6. In which century did Otto Lilienthal make the first controlled glider flights: the ninth or 19th century?
Answer: The 19th century

7. How many wings does a monoplane have: two or four?
Answer: Two

8. Which "G" is a country, home to Otto Lilienthal?
Answer: Germany

9. Jean-François Pilâtre was the first man to fly. True or false?
Answer: True

10. Was the first powered airplane flight in Europe or the United States?
Answer: The U.S.

11. Which great 16th-century Italian artist and thinker designed a glider that was never built?
Answer: Leonardo da Vinci

12. Which "M" were brothers who built the first manned aircraft?
Answer: Montgolfier

Level 3

13. What was the last name of Wilbur and Orville, who designed the first-ever heavier-than-air powered aircraft?
Answer: Wright

14. What was the Wright brothers' aircraft called?
Answer: The Wright Flyer

15. What did the first heavier-than-air powered aircraft use as fuel?
Answer: Gasoline

16. In which century did the first-ever manned aircraft take off: the 16th, 17th, or 18th century?
Answer: The 18th century

17. Who made the first-ever powered flight?
Answer: Henri Giffard

18. What was the nationality of the person who made the first-ever powered flight?
Answer: French

ANSWERS: Sailing

Level 1

1. Sailboats use the wind to push them along. True or false?
Answer: True

2. Are boats kept moored in a marina, a merino, or a mariner?
Answer: A marina

3. What type of jackets do people wear to keep them afloat in the water?
Answer: Life jackets

4. Do any sailboats have engines?
Answer: Yes

5. What suit keeps windsurfers warm?
Answer: A wet suit

6. A rudder is used to help steer a boat. True or false?
Answer: True

7. What "Y" is a large sailboat used for pleasure?
Answer: Yacht

Level 2

8. Which were invented first: square sails or triangular sails?
Answer: Square sails

9. What "P" is the left-hand side of a boat and a place where ships dock?
Answer: Port

10. What is the word for the rear of a boat?
Answer: The stern

11. BROAD ARTS can be rearranged to give what word for the right-hand side of a boat?
Answer: Starboard

12. Boats with square sails can only go in the same direction as the wind. True or false?
Answer: True

13. How many hulls do trimarans have?
Answer: Three

14. What is a boat with two hulls called?
Answer: A catamaran

15. What are small, open boats without cabins called?
Answer: Dinghies

16. What "W" are people who sail standing up on a board?
Answer: Windsurfers

Level 3

17. What part of a boat helps keep it from tipping over?
Answer: The keel

18. Which Mediterranean island was home to the seafaring Minoans?
Answer: Crete

19. When did ancient sailing ships use their oars?
Answer: When they wanted to go forward against the wind

ANSWERS: Submarines

Level 1
1. Does the word "submarine" literally mean "under the sea" or "above the mountains"?
   Answer: Under the sea
2. Is a torpedo a type of weapon or a running shoe?
   Answer: A type of weapon
3. What "D" is the word for people who explore underwater?
   Answer: Divers
4. LATIN CAT can be rearranged to give the name of which ocean?
   Answer: Atlantic

Level 2
5. Which country's submarines were known as U-boats?
   Answer: Germany's
6. Are there any submarines that are driven by nuclear power?
   Answer: Yes
7. What is the name for the spinning objects that push submarines through the water?
   Answer: Propellers
8. Can submarines attack boats that are on the surface?
   Answer: Yes
9. Are research submarines called submersibles or submissives?
   Answer: Submersibles
10. What "D" is a type of fuel commonly used in submarines?
    Answer: Diesel
11. What is the name for the tanks that fill with seawater when a submarine descends?
    Answer: Ballast tanks
12. A bathyscaphe is a type of radar system. True or false?
    Answer: False
13. What do the letters ROV stand for?
    Answer: Remotely operated vehicle
14. SPICE ROPE can be rearranged to give the name of what device used by submarine crews to see above the water?
    Answer: Periscope

Level 3
15. Where is the Mariana Trench, the deepest point on Earth?
    Answer: The Pacific Ocean
16. What was the name of the bathyscaphe that first carried people to the bottom of the Mariana Trench?
    Answer: Trieste
17. What was the name of the manned submersible that first explored the wreck of the *Titanic*?
    Answer: Alvin
18. Which ocean liner was torpedoed and sunk by a German U-boat on May 7, 1915?
    Answer: RMS Lusitania

ANSWERS: Household inventions

Level 1
1. Would you put bread in a toaster or a dishwasher?
   Answer: A toaster
2. What "K" is used for heating water?
   Answer: Kettle
3. Which was invented first, the electric washing machine or the food processor?
   Answer: The electric washing machine

Level 2
4. Which invention is usually credited to John Logie Baird?
   Answer: Television
5. SHARED WISH can be rearranged to give the name of what household appliance?
   Answer: Dishwasher
6. Did the automatic cutout on an electric kettle appear in 1890, 1930, or 1989?
   Answer: 1930
7. Which was invented first: the electric washing machine or the dishwasher?
   Answer: The electric washing machine
8. Which household object is usually associated with Thomas Edison?
   Answer: The electric lightbulb
9. People only started to use zippers in the 1940s. True or false?
   Answer: False
10. Which handy implement was invented by Laszlo Biro?
    Answer: The ballpoint pen
11. The aerofoam extinguisher is used on what type of fires?
    Answer: Gas and oil
12. SCOOPS RED ROOF can be rearranged to give the name of what kitchen appliance?
    Answer: Food processor
13. In which decade of the 20th century did microwave ovens first go on sale?
    Answer: The 1960s

Level 3
14. In what year was the first television picture transmitted?
    Answer: 1925
15. James Murray Spangler invented the first portable what?
    Answer: Vacuum cleaner
16. What did Alexandre Godefoy invent?
    Answer: The hair dryer
17. Which kitchen appliance was developed from an earlier invention called the magnetron?
    Answer: The microwave oven
18. Who invented the sewing machine?
    Answer: Elias Howe

ANSWERS: Robots

Level 1

1. Are there any robots that work in factories?
   Answer: Yes
2. Do robots ever get tired?
   Answer: No
3. Are there any robots that can work underwater?
   Answer: Yes
4. ODD SIR can be rearranged to give what name for robots such as R2-D2?
   Answer: Droids
5. Robots can only do one thing at a time. True or false?
   Answer: False

Level 2

6. Are there any robots that can play the piano?
   Answer: Yes
7. Which series of movies starred the robot C-3PO?
   Answer: Star Wars
8. What "C" is programmed with the information that is needed to make robots operate?
   Answer: Computer
9. LEWDING can be rearranged to give the name of what task performed by robots?
   Answer: Welding
10. Which have traveled farthest from Earth: robots or humans?
    Answer: Robots
11. Solar panels are used to capture energy from which source?
    Answer: The Sun
12. Can robots perform sign language?
    Answer: Yes
13. Which planet is currently being explored by robots?
    Answer: Mars
14. What "M" is the word for doing more than one job at a time?
    Answer: Multitasking
15. Can robots be programmed to detonate bombs?
    Answer: Yes

Level 3

16. The word "robot" comes from which language?
    Answer: Czech
17. Which country developed the WABOT-2 robot?
    Answer: Japan
18. In what year was the animated movie *Robots* released?
    Answer: 2005

ANSWERS: Computers and video games

Level 1

1. What "I" is the network that links computers all over the world?
   Answer: The Internet
2. Does "PC" stand for perfect computer or personal computer?
   Answer: Personal computer
3. What is a computer that is small enough to fit in the hand called: a handbag, a handheld, or a handshake?
   Answer: A handheld
4. What "M" is a small, furry animal and an object that attaches to a computer?
   Answer: A mouse
5. What is stored in MP3 files?
   Answer: Music

Level 2

6. Where were computer games played before people had home computers?
   Answer: In video arcades
7. Can people play computer games while they are on the move?
   Answer: Yes
8. What type of computer is the word "Mac" short for?
   Answer: Macintosh
9. Do most handheld game machines take cartridges or disks?
   Answer: Cartridges
10. Is the information in a computer held in the hard drive, printer, or mouse?
    Answer: In the hard drive
11. What "B" is the computer equipment used to put information onto a CD?
    Answer: Burner
12. Is a computer keyboard a peripheral or a profiterole?
    Answer: A peripheral
13. What "V" is put in front of the word "reality" to describe lifelike situations produced by computers?
    Answer: Virtual
14. What "H" do you wear when playing a virtual-reality game?
    Answer: A headset
15. TOP PAL can be rearranged to give what name for a portable computer?
    Answer: Laptop

Level 3

16. Which would you use to store data: a CD-RAM, a CD-REM, or a CD-ROM?
    Answer: A CD-ROM
17. What connects a home computer to the Internet?
    Answer: A telephone line
18. What type of files would you put onto an iPod?
    Answer: MP3 files

ANSWERS: Telephones

Level 1

1. What "T" is a written message sent by a cell phone?
Answer: Text

2. Were the first cell phones bigger or smaller than cell phones today?
Answer: Bigger

3. Do most modern telephones have rotating dials or buttons?
Answer: Buttons

4. Do cell phones send messages using microwaves, water waves, or Mexican waves?
Answer: Microwaves

5. Are there cell phones that can connect to the Internet?
Answer: Yes

Level 2

6. Did the world's first telephone have touch-tone dialing?
Answer: No

7. In what century was the telephone invented: ninth, 19th, or 21st?
Answer: The 19th century

8. SAME CAR can be rearranged to spell what extra feature of some cell phones?
Answer: Cameras

9. HOME CUT PIE can be rearranged to spell what part of a telephone that you speak into?
Answer: Mouthpiece

10. What "E" is the place where telephone calls are connected?
Answer: Exchange

11. What name is given to the people who used to connect telephone calls?
Answer: Operators

12. How many names were in the first-ever telephone directory: 50, 500, or 5,000?
Answer: 50

13. What "T" was a type of coded message used before telephones were invented?
Answer: Telegram

Level 3

14. How did people generate the electricity to power early phones?
Answer: By winding a handle on the side of the phone

15. Who invented the telephone?
Answer: Alexander Graham Bell

16. In which country was Alexander Graham Bell born?
Answer: Scotland

17. Who invented the carbon-granule microphone?
Answer: Thomas Edison

18. Which was invented first: the fax machine or the telephone?
Answer: The fax machine

19. In what year did rotating dials appear: 1886, 1896, or 1906?
Answer: 1896

ANSWERS: Discoveries

Level 1

1. What type of food is said to have fallen on Sir Isaac Newton's head, giving him the idea for his most famous theory?
Answer: An apple

2. What "W" turns around and around, allowing vehicles to move?
Answer: A wheel

3. IT GRAVY can be rearranged to give the name of what force that pulls objects toward the ground?
Answer: Gravity

Level 2

4. Which mathematician living in ancient Greece shouted, "Eureka!" when he was taking a bath?
Answer: Archimedes

5. What nationality was Sir Isaac Newton?
Answer: English

6. In which century did the first cars with gasoline engines appear?
Answer: In the 19th century

7. Michael Faraday was an American scientist. True or false?
Answer: False (he was English)

8. What "S" was used to power the earliest cars?
Answer: Steam

9. Karl Benz was a pioneer of the motorcar. True or false?
Answer: True

10. SPICY HITS can be rearranged to give the name of what type of scientist?
Answer: Physicist

11. Who devised the theory of relativity?
Answer: Albert Einstein

12. Was the wheel invented more than 3,000 years ago?
Answer: Yes

13. What "M" did Michael Faraday help us understand better?
Answer: Magnetism

14. What nationality was Nicolas Cugnot, who built the first car?
Answer: French

15. By what three letters is deoxyribonucleic acid usually known?
Answer: DNA

Level 3

16. In which modern country are the ruins of the city of Uruk?
Answer: Iraq

17. Which two scientists are usually credited with discovering the double helix of deoxyribonucleic acid?
Answer: Francis Crick and James Watson

18. In the formula $E = mc^2$, what does "E" stand for?
Answer: Energy

ANSWERS: Ancient Egypt

Level 1

1. Which river flows through Egypt?
   Answer: The Nile river
2. What did the ancient Egyptians call their leader?
   Answer: The pharaoh
3. Did Egyptians believe in life after death?
   Answer: Yes
4. What was made of wool or human hair?
   Answer: Wigs
5. What were Egyptian clothes made from?
   Answer: Linen

Level 2

6. What form of writing did the Egyptians use?
   Answer: Hieroglyphics
7. What was papyrus made from?
   Answer: Reeds
8. What was usually buried with an Egyptian's body?
   Answer: Their clothes and furniture and food and drinks
9. How did the Egyptians usually decorate their coffins?
   Answer: With a portrait of the dead person
10. What was "Opening the Mouth"?
    Answer: A ceremony performed by priests at a dead pharaoh's tomb
11. What is the biggest pyramid called?
    Answer: The Great Pyramid of Giza
12. What flower was the symbol of the Nile river?
    Answer: The lotus

Level 3

13. Which part of the body was used to measure a cubit: the leg, the foot, or the forearm?
    Answer: The forearm
14. How did the Egyptians transport a pharaoh's body?
    Answer: On a funeral boat
15. What did Egyptians use to dry a body when embalming it?
    Answer: Salt
16. What animal is associated with the Egyptian god of kings?
    Answer: The hawk
17. What did the priest say during a death ceremony?
    Answer: "You live again, you live again forever"
18. For how long did the pharaohs rule Egypt?
    Answer: For 3,000 years
19. Who is buried in the Great Pyramid of Giza?
    Answer: The pharaoh Cheops (Khufu)

ANSWERS: Ancient Greece

Level 1

1. What "M" is one of the seas around Greece?
   Answer: The Mediterrean Sea
2. Who was the ruler of the Greek gods?
   Answer: Zeus
3. Where were the ancient Olympic Games held?
   Answer: Olympia
4. Was the Trojan horse made out of stone or wood?
   Answer: Wood
5. The Greeks had slaves. True or false?
   Answer: True

Level 2

6. A SPRAT can be rearranged to give the name of what Greek city-state?
   Answer: Sparta
7. What did women use in order to weave fabrics for clothes?
   Answer: A loom
8. At around what age did women get married?
   Answer: 15 years old
9. Who hid inside the Trojan horse?
   Answer: Greek soldiers
10. SNOOD PIE can be rearranged to give the name of what Greek god?
    Answer: Poseidon
11. What material did the Greeks use to make bricks?
    Answer: Mud
12. How did wealthy Greeks travel on land: by horse or by carriage?
    Answer: By horse
13. The Greek Empire included many islands. True or false?
    Answer: True
14. When traveling in Greece, people slept outside. True or false?
    Answer: True
15. Where were the gods said to live?
    Answer: On Mount Olympus

Level 3

16. In which modern country was the ancient city of Troy?
    Answer: Turkey
17. What did a winner receive at the Olympic Games?
    Answer: A crown of olive leaves
18. What was a chiton?
    Answer: A basic woman's dress made out of a single rectangular piece of cloth
19. Where in the home did the Greeks have an altar?
    Answer: In the courtyard
20. Who was the goddess of the home?
    Answer: Hestia

ANSWERS: The Colosseum

Level 1
1. What famous gladiator led a revolt of slaves?
   Answer: Spartacus
2. There were elephants in the Colosseum. True or false?
   Answer: True
3. What signal did the crowd give for a gladiator to die?
   Answer: Thumbs down
4. CUT ROSE can be rearranged to give the name of what type of gladiator?
   Answer: Secutor

Level 2
5. In what part of the Colosseum were the gladiators and animals kept?
   Answer: In underground chambers
6. Which emperor often fought at the Colosseum?
   Answer: Commodus
7. What was a *bestiarius*?
   Answer: A man trained to fight animals
8. What did a *retiarius* use to catch his opponent?
   Answer: A net and a three-pronged spear
9. Who were thrown to the animals?
   Answer: Christians, criminals, and slaves
10. What type of gladiator wore a helmet decorated with a fish?
    Answer: A murmillo
11. How many years did it take to build the Colosseum: ten, 20, or 30?
    Answer: ten
12. The *venationes* were Roman soldiers. True or false?
    Answer: False

Level 3
13. What did a freed gladiator receive?
    Answer: A bone tablet, inscribed with his name, and a gift of coins
14. How many people could attend games at the Colosseum?
    Answer: 50,000 people
15. When were the first gladiator games held?
    Answer: In 264 B.C.
16. How did the Colosseum get its name?
    Answer: From the nearby colossus (statue) of Nero
17. How many times did Commodus fight at the Colosseum?
    Answer: 735 times
18. How many animals were killed in the first celebrations at the Colosseum?
    Answer: 5,000

ANSWERS: Medieval life

Level 1
1. A banquet is a type of battle. True or false?
   Answer: False (it is a feast)
2. People ate meals in the great hall. True or false?
   Answer: True
3. Was a jongleur a person or a musical instrument?
   Answer: A person
4. Who owned the land in medieval times?
   Answer: The king
5. Who taught the children of noblemen: priests or servants?
   Answer: Priests

Level 2
6. Who rented land from noblemen?
   Answer: Knights and lords
7. What were jongleurs called in England?
   Answer: Gleemen
8. What was the name of the system by which land was given out?
   Answer: The feudal system
9. What was the center of a castle called?
   Answer: The keep
10. Where did important people sit during a banquet?
    Answer: At the high table
11. How were castle floors kept warm?
    Answer: They were covered with reeds
12. Where were medieval girls taught?
    Answer: At home
13. What was the cup board for?
    Answer: Displaying the lord's cups and plates
14. What was used to help rid the castle floor of bad smells?
    Answer: Spices

Level 3
15. What language did the sons of nobles learn?
    Answer: Latin
16. Why did people like to hear music while they were eating?
    Answer: They believed that it aided digestion
17. Where did village boys learn trades?
    Answer: At local guilds
18. What were trenchers?
    Answer: Wooden boards that diners ate from

ANSWERS: Knights

Level 1

1. What "L" was a weapon used by knights on horseback?
   Answer: A lance
2. What was a battering ram used for?
   Answer: To weaken castle walls
3. RED GAG can be rearranged to give the name of what weapon used by knights?
   Answer: Dagger
4. Knights only ever fought on horseback. True or false?
   Answer: False

Level 2

5. What did an esquire become during a dubbing ceremony?
   Answer: A knight
6. What was a mace?
   Answer: A heavy club
7. How did a jousting knight knock his opponent off his horse?
   Answer: With a dull lance
8. What type of missiles did a mangonel shoot?
   Answer: Rocks
9. Did a knight use a crossbow or a longbow?
   Answer: He used both
10. Why did jousting begin?
    Answer: As battle training
11. What weapon was used to shoot bolts at a castle?
    Answer: A ballista
12. How could knights tell each other apart in battle?
    Answer: By the coats of arms on their surcoats
13. What is a trebuchet?
    Answer: A siege weapon used for hurling stones at castle walls
14. How could attackers force the defenders of a castle to surrender?
    Answer: By starving them

Level 3

15. What was the name of the fee paid by knights who did not want to fight?
    Answer: Scutage
16. What was a bevor?
    Answer: A piece of armor that protected a knight's neck
17. How was an esquire dubbed?
    Answer: His lord tapped him on the shoulder with the flat blade of his sword
18. By which century had knights begun wearing plated armor?
    Answer: The 15th century

ANSWERS: The Renaissance

Level 1

1. Does the word "Renaissance" mean "rebirth" or "revolting"?
   Answer: It means "rebirth"
2. BLAMER can be rearranged to give the name of what material used by Renaissance sculptors?
   Answer: Marble
3. Was Donatello a painter or a sculptor?
   Answer: A sculptor
4. The lute is a musical instrument. True or false?
   Answer: True

Level 2

5. Ghiberti was a Renaissance philosopher. True or false?
   Answer: False
6. Where was block printing invented?
   Answer: China
7. What was the lira da braccio used for?
   Answer: For accompanying poems
8. What painting featured the ancient philosophers Plato and Aristotle?
   Answer: The School of Athens
9. What was the first-ever mass-produced book?
   Answer: A Bible
10. HARE PAL can be rearranged to give the name of what Renaissance artist?
    Answer: Raphael
11. What nationality was Erasmus?
    Answer: Dutch
12. Which two civilizations influenced Renaissance artists?
    Answer: Greek and Roman
13. What is the name of the leather pad that applied the ink in the first European printing press?
    Answer: An ink ball
14. What type of philosophers thought that moral lessons could be learned from ancient texts?
    Answer: Humanists

Level 3

15. What "B" was a famous Renaissance architect?
    Answer: Brunelleschi
16. In what year was the printing press invented in Europe?
    Answer: 1440
17. The Renaissance lasted until which century?
    Answer: The 17th century
18. Who invented the printing press in Europe?
    Answer: Johannes Gutenberg

ANSWERS: The age of exploration

Level 1

1. Was Sir Francis Drake an Englishman or a Spaniard?
   Answer: An Englishman
2. What was Columbus' largest ship called: the *Santa Maria*, the *Santa Anna*, or the *Santa Barbara*?
   Answer: The Santa Maria
3. Francisco Pizarro conquered the Incas. True or false?
   Answer: True
4. From which country was Bartholomew Dias?
   Answer: Portugal

Level 2

5. Which did Magellan discover: the Indian Ocean or the Pacific Ocean?
   Answer: The Pacific Ocean
6. How many men were in the crew of Columbus' largest ship: 30, 40, or 60?
   Answer: 40
7. Who sent Columbus to find a route to China?
   Answer: The king of Spain
8. Did Dias or da Gama sail around the southern tip of Africa?
   Answer: Dias
9. Who reached India in 1498?
   Answer: Vasco da Gama
10. What was Zheng He the first to do?
    Answer: Use a compass on a sea voyage
11. What were the names of Columbus' two caravels?
    Answer: The Niña and the Pinta
12. What was a back staff used for?
    Answer: Measuring the angle of the Sun
13. Why did Ferdinand Magellan not reach his final destination?
    Answer: He was killed in the Philippines
14. What did Columbus believe he had reached?
    Answer: The Far East
15. What part of the world did the Incas rule?
    Answer: The western coast of South America (now Peru)

Level 3

16. On which island did Columbus land?
    Answer: San Salvador
17. What was discovered in 1911?
    Answer: Machu Picchu
18. What is a nao?
    Answer: A merchant ship
19. When did a ship first sail all the way around the world?
    Answer: 1522

ANSWERS: World War I

Level 1

1. What large machine was used for the first time in World War I?
   Answer: The tank
2. What is a dogfight?
   Answer: A battle in the air between two or more aircraft
3. What was the area between enemy trenches called?
   Answer: No-man's-land
4. A grenade is a weapon. True or false?
   Answer: True

Level 2

5. What type of protection did soldiers have against gas?
   Answer: Gas masks
6. For what purpose were horses used?
   Answer: To pull ambulances and weaponry
7. Which "J" was a major battle fought at sea?
   Answer: The Battle of Jutland
8. Where was the Western Front?
   Answer: In Belgium and France
9. What name is used for a trained marksman who tries to shoot lone soldiers?
   Answer: A sniper
10. What weapon could be attached to a rifle?
    Answer: A bayonet
11. How many lives were lost in the war: more than 7.5 million, more than 8.5 million, or more than ten million?
    Answer: More than 8.5 million
12. In which country is Jutland?
    Answer: Denmark
13. What lined the tops of trenches?
    Answer: Sandbags
14. What weapons were installed in fighter planes?
    Answer: Machine guns

Level 3

15. In what year was poison gas first used?
    Answer: 1915
16. Which model of tank was the first one strong enough to withstand antitank rifles?
    Answer: The British Mark IV
17. What was the name given to the British soldiers who trained horses?
    Answer: Roughriders
18. What German fighter plane was considered to be the best fighter plane of the war?
    Answer: The Fokker D.VII

ANSWERS: Summer Olympics

Level 1

1. How many rings are there in the Olympic symbol?
Answer: Five

2. Which Olympic sport features a 16-ft. (5-m)-long springy pole?
Answer: Pole vaulting

3. How often are the Summer Olympic Games held?
Answer: Every four years

4. Do equestrian events use a horse, a bicycle, or a pistol?
Answer: A horse

5. Which type of swimming race is longer: a sprint or an endurance race?
Answer: An endurance race

Level 2

6. Is a marathon race 20km, 42km, or 50km long?
Answer: 42km

7. What is the name of a competitor in a judo fight?
Answer: A judoka

8. Which horse-based sport takes three days to complete?
Answer: Eventing

9. What is the name of the building in which track cyclists compete?
Answer: A velodrome

10. Who set a world record of 6.14m for the pole vault?
Answer: Sergey Bubka

11. What is the longest distance race in track events at the Olympics?
Answer: The 50km racewalk

12. How many Olympics has Jeannie Longo-Ciprelli appeared at: three, four, or six?
Answer: Six

13. In which sport did Mark Spitz win seven gold medals in 1972?
Answer: Swimming

Level 3

14. How long is a steeplechase race at the Olympics?
Answer: 3,000m

15. When was judo first included in the Olympics?
Answer: 1964

16. How much shorter is a woman's judo bout than a man's?
Answer: One minute

17. What fraction of the total gold medals for judo did Japan win in 2004?
Answer: Half

ANSWERS: Gymnastics

Level 1

1. When do athletes warm up?
Answer: Before competing

2. What are people who perform gymnastics called?
Answer: Gymnasts

3. How many handles does a pommel horse have?
Answer: Two

4. Are the rings used only by men or by both men and women?
Answer: Only by men

5. What do some athletes dust their hands with to help with their grip?
Answer: Chalk

Level 2

6. In gymnastics, how many events do female athletes compete in?
Answer: Four

7. Did rhythmic gymnastics first appear in the Olympics in 1932, 1968, or 1984?
Answer: 1984

8. How many items of equipment are there in rhythmic gymnastics?
Answer: Five

9. Was the first person to get the highest possible score in artistic gymnastics at the Olympics a man or a woman?
Answer: A woman

10. What is the highest possible score given to a competitor for one routine: 10, 15, or 20?
Answer: 10

11. What "H" is a piece of rhythmic gymnastics equipment?
Answer: Hoop

12. What are the two hoops that hang above the ground called?
Answer: Rings

13. What type of gymnastics is performed to music?
Answer: Rhythmic gymnastics

14. How many panels of judges score rhythmic gymnastics?
Answer: Three

Level 3

15. How high are the parallel bars?
Answer: 5.7 ft. (1.75m) high

16. Who was the first person to get the highest possible score in artistic gymnastics at the Olympics?
Answer: Nadia Comaneci

17. Who invented the parallel bars?
Answer: Friedrich Jahn

18. From which gymnastics apparatus would a gymnast dismount?
Answer: The pommel horse

ANSWERS: Winter sports

Level 1

1. How many skis does a skier use?
    Answer: Two
2. Do speed skaters race downhill, around a track, or along a road?
    Answer: Around a track
3. Which country invented ice hockey?
    Answer: Canada
4. Which is also known as cross-country skiing: Nordic or downhill?
    Answer: Nordic skiing
5. What name is given to someone who teaches others how to ski?
    Answer: Ski instructor

Level 2

6. In which winter sport do players try to hit a puck into a goal?
    Answer: Ice hockey
7. What is the front of a snowboard called?
    Answer: The nose
8. Downhill skiing is part of the Winter Olympics. True or false?
    Answer: True
9. What is the name of the sticks that skiers hold in their hands?
    Answer: Ski poles
10. In which winter sport can competitors reach a speed of 37 mph (60km/h) as they race around a track?
    Answer: Speed skating
11. Are there six, nine, or 11 players per team in ice hockey?
    Answer: Six
12. Do Nordic or slalom skiers race a zigzagging course?
    Answer: Slalom skiers
13. What is the back of a snowboard called?
    Answer: The tail
14. How many periods are there in an ice hockey game?
    Answer: Three
15. The biathlon involves rifle shooting and what type of skiing?
    Answer: Nordic skiing
16. In what year did snowboarding become an Olympic sport?
    Answer: 1998

Level 3

17. Who can travel the fastest: speed skaters or downhill skiers?
    Answer: Downhill skiers
18. What object attaches ski boots to skis?
    Answer: Bindings
19. Which skis are shorter and wider: Nordic skis or downhill skis?
    Answer: Downhill skis
20. What is the name of the player who guards a goal in ice hockey?
    Answer: The goalkeeper

ANSWERS: Baseball

Level 1

1. Baseball gloves are made out of cotton. True or false?
    Answer: False (they are made out of leather)
2. How many bases are there on a baseball field: four, 14, or 20?
    Answer: Four
3. A changeup is a type of baseball bat. True or false?
    Answer: False (it is a type of fast pitch)
4. Does the catcher stand just behind the batter or just in front of him?
    Answer: Just behind him

Level 2

5. Which is covered in dirt: the infield or the outfield?
    Answer: The infield
6. What "M" is a piece of baseball equipment worn on the hand?
    Answer: A mitt
7. People played baseball in the 1800s. True or false?
    Answer: True
8. Is Yankee Stadium in San Francisco, New York City, or Los Angeles?
    Answer: New York City
9. MOTEL HEAP can be rearranged to give the name of which place on a baseball field?
    Answer: Home plate
10. Who would "bunt" a ball: a batter, a pitcher, or a fielder?
    Answer: A batter
11. What "F" is a type of baseball pitch, thrown fast?
    Answer: Fastball
12. Which player wears a mask made out of metal?
    Answer: The catcher
13. What baseball team plays at Fenway Park?
    Answer: The Boston Red Sox
14. How far away does the pitcher stand from the batter: 60.5 ft. (18m), 70.5 ft. (21m), or 80.5 ft. (25m)?
    Answer: 60.5 ft. (18m)

Level 3

15. In what town is Abner Doubleday said to have invented baseball?
    Answer: Cooperstown, NY
16. In which stadium do the St. Louis Cardinals play?
    Answer: Busch Stadium

ANSWERS:
Art and painting

Level 1

1. The famous artist Michelangelo came from Italy. True or false?
   Answer: True
2. What was van Gogh's first name?
   Answer: Vincent
3. In what country are the famous Lascaux cave paintings?
   Answer: France
4. Were sculptures, cave paintings, or frescoes made on damp plaster?
   Answer: Frescoes
5. The Lascaux cave paintings feature paintings of reindeer. True or false?
   Answer: True

Level 2

6. What part of an egg was used by prehistoric cave painters?
   Answer: The white
7. Can you name either of the colors that were often used by the ancient Greeks to decorate their pottery?
   Answer: Red or black
8. Do artists who paint frescoes have to work slowly or quickly?
   Answer: Quickly
9. Does tempera or oil paint produce richer colors?
   Answer: Oil paint
10. Did Michelangelo paint a fresco on the doors, the walls, or the ceiling of the Sistine Chapel?
    Answer: The ceiling
11. From what was Michelangelo's sculpture of Moses carved?
    Answer: Marble
12. Does oil paint or tempera paint dry more slowly?
    Answer: Oil paint
13. What part of an egg was used to make tempera paints?
    Answer: The yolk

Level 3

14. Blam! is a famous pop art painting. Who painted it?
    Answer: Roy Lichtenstein
15. In what century did Michelangelo carve a sculpture of Moses?
    Answer: The 16th century
16. How old was van Gogh when he painted *Starry Night*?
    Answer: 36
17. In which decade did pop art first appear?
    Answer: In the 1950s
18. Are the prehistoric paintings in the Lascaux caves around 15,000, 16,000, or 17,000 years old?
    Answer: Around 17,000 years old

ANSWERS:
Ballet

Level 1

1. Do most ballet dancers start as children, teenagers, or adults?
   Answer: As children
2. Do ballets take place in a rink, a court, or in a theater?
   Answer: A theater
3. Do male ballet dancers wear makeup?
   Answer: Yes
4. Is a tutu a ballet shoe, a skirt, or a type of ballet move?
   Answer: A skirt

Level 2

5. What type of musician often plays during ballet classes?
   Answer: A pianist
6. In *Swan Lake*, what part of the body does a ballerina move to look like wings?
   Answer: The arms
7. Before a show, where do dancers put on their makeup?
   Answer: In the dressing room
8. A port de bras exercise involves the movement of which parts of the body?
   Answer: The arms
9. How many basic positions are there for the feet in ballet?
   Answer: Five
10. The heels touch together in which position: first, second, or third?
    Answer: First
11. ASK LAWNE can be rearranged to give the name of which ballet?
    Answer: Swan Lake
12. Why do dancers wear leg warmers when they practice?
    Answer: To keep their muscles warm and to prevent strains and injuries
13. What term means "dancing on the tips of the toes"?
    Answer: Pointe work
14. In a ballet what is the break between acts called?
    Answer: The intermission
15. A major ballet may need as many as 30, 300, or 3,000 costumes?
    Answer: 300 costumes

Level 3

16. Which country does the ballet *Swan Lake* come from?
    Answer: Russia
17. What term means the leading female dancer in a ballet company?
    Answer: Prima ballerina
18. What "O" is the queen of the swans in *Swan Lake*?
    Answer: Odette

ANSWERS: Architecture

ANSWERS: Movies and TV

Architecture

Level 1
1. Who built the Parthenon: the Greeks, Egyptians, or Romans?
Answer: The Greeks
2. What is the name given to the giant buildings used to bury the rulers (pharaohs) in ancient Egypt?
Answer: Pyramids
3. Were the first bricks made of mud and clay or cement and gravel?
Answer: Mud and clay
4. Are the pyramids of ancient Egypt made of mud, wood, or stone?
Answer: Stone
5. Were the first bricks made solid by setting them on fire, letting them dry in the sun, or freezing them?
Answer: Letting them dry in the sun

Level 2
6. Which civilization invented concrete?
Answer: The Romans
7. Was the Parthenon built of granite, cement, or marble?
Answer: Marble
8. In which city is the Parthenon?
Answer: Athens
9. Why does Hardwick Hall have many windows?
Answer: As a sign of wealth
10. Did the White House get water pipes or gas lighting installed first?
Answer: Water pipes
11. Did the Gothic style of architecture begin in Europe, Asia, or Africa?
Answer: Europe
12. What is the name of wooden strips that are filled in with daub?
Answer: Wattles
13. Who built Hardwick Hall?
Answer: Bess of Hardwick

Level 3
14. What are the architect's detailed plans for a building called?
Answer: Blueprints
15. Which famous building did James Hoban rebuild?
Answer: The White House
16. The Parthenon was a temple for the worship of which goddess?
Answer: Athena
17. What is a flying buttress?
Answer: A special side support
18. During which century did Gothic architecture first appear?
Answer: The 12th century

Movies and TV

Level 1
1. Were the first TV broadcasts black-and-white or color?
Answer: Black-and-white
2. What "D" is the person in charge of the filmmaking process?
Answer: The director
3. What name is given to someone who interviews people for the news?
Answer: Reporter
4. What word describes people who play characters and appear in movies?
Answer: Actors
5. What word describes the written-down version of a movie?
Answer: The screenplay

Level 2
6. Who are the three people needed in a news team?
Answer: Reporter, camera operator, and sound recordist
7. What word describes news reporting that is transmitted as the events happen?
Answer: Live
8. Was the first movie with sound *Casablanca*, *The Jazz Singer*, or *Snow White*?
Answer: The Jazz Singer
9. WOOLY HOLD can be rearranged to give the name of what huge movie industry based in the U.S.?
Answer: Hollywood
10. Near which big American city is Hollywood located?
Answer: Los Angeles, California
11. What nickname is given to India's movie industry?
Answer: Bollywood
12. What name is given to 24-hour news programs?
Answer: Rolling news

Level 3
13. Was Telstar the name of an early television or a satellite?
Answer: A satellite
14. In what year was the first "talking" movie made?
Answer: 1927
15. In 1962 what percentage of U.S. homes had a television?
Answer: 90 percent
16. In what year was the first TV signal sent by satellite?
Answer: 1962
17. What word is used for sending programs out from a TV station?
Answer: Broadcasting
18. Which Asian country has one of the largest movie industries in the world?
Answer: India

Index

Acknowledgments

The publisher would like to thank the following for permission to reproduce their material. Every care has been taken to trace copyright holders. However, if there have been unintentional omissions or failure to trace copyright holders, we apologize and will, if informed, endeavor to make corrections in any future edition.

b = bottom, c = center, l = left, r = right, t = top

PHOTOGRAPHS

16bc Corbis/Tim Davis; 27br Corbis/Staffan Widstrand; 35cr Corbis/Kit Houghton; 60c NASA; 70bl Corbis/Frank Tusch/zefa; 73t Siemens Ltd; 86tr Corbis/Dann Tardiff; 89cl Bradbury & Williams/Roy Williams; 89br Bradbury & Williams/Roy Williams; 94tr Robert Harding; 116cr Swedish Travel and Tourism Council; 121br Corbis/KIPA; 125br Corbis/William Manning, BR; 125cr Corbis/Eric Crichton

ILLUSTRATIONS

Susanna Addario 88cr, 88bl; Lisa Alderson 4–5b, 8b; Marion Appleton 121bl; Artists Partners 83br, 127bl; Mike Atkinson 75tr; Julian Baker 64cl, 103cl; Julian Baum 62c; Owain Bell 91cr; Mark Bergin 79cl, 101tl, 102cl, 112bl; Richard Berridge (Specs Art) 35tr; Gary Bines 61cr, 85t; Brighton Illustration Agency 32c; Mike Buckley/Malcolm Parchment 118cl, 118br, 119t; Peter Bull 44tc, 69cl; John Butler 31bl; Martin Camm 21cr; Robin Carter (Wildlife Art Agency) 67tl; Jim Channell 20l, 33b, 48c; Kuo Kang Chen 82b; Harry Clow 54tr; Gino D'Achille (Artist Partners) 56–57b, 103cr; Peter Dennis (Linda Rogers) 19tr, 32tr, 46–47t, 72tr, 98tr, 101cl, 102tr, 109cl; Kay Dixey 119cl; Richard Draper 17c, 47c; Dan Escott 100bl; James Field 55t; Chris Forsey 9cr, 9br, 11cr, 12tr, 12–13b, 13t, 30b, 48tr, 49br, 52–53c, 52bc, 53tr, 59b, 60–61b, 63b, 64tr, 65t, 65cr, 66tr, 81tr, 106tr, 120cr, 120br, 124tr; Mark Franklin 46br; Oliver Frey 105tr; Luigi Galante 120bl; Tony Gibbons 80bl; Jeremy Gower 42cr, 85cr; Lindsay Graham (Linden Artists) 34tl, 35bl; Craig Greenwood (Wildlife Art Agency) 14tr; Ray Grinaway 16cl, 22–23c, 33cr, 66c, 67cr, 67bl; Nick Hall 43tr; Alan Hancock 70tr; Alan Harris 25cr; Gary Hincks 51c, 106–107c; Christian Hook (Linden Artists) 123cr, 127tl; Richard Hook 54b, 98cr; Andre Hrydziusko 69tr; Biz Hull 122cl, 122bl; Ian Jackson (Wildlife Art) 7b, 26b, 28–29b, 39c, 55b; Rob Jakeway/Bill Donohoe 64–65b; John James 76–77b, 106bl; Ron Jobson 74cl, 83tl, 83tr, 83c; Michael Johnson 51b; Peter Jones (John Martin) 106cl; Peter Kelly 43c; Roger Kent (Garden Studio) 9t; Martin Knowldon (Virgil Pomfret) 28tr, 28c; Mike Lacey (SGA) 56cr, 57tl, 107tl, 116tr, 117tl, 119b; Linden Artists 22bl, 31tr, 108tr; Bernard Long (Temple Rogers) 11t; 48b; Kevin Maddison 24cl, 50–51c, 51tl, 79tl, 79b, 97cl; Mainline Design 23br; Shirley Mallinsen 12cl; Maltings Partnership 72bl, 82c, 113tr, 87tr; John Marshall (Temple Art) 74tr; Josephine Martin 10tr; David McAllister 79tr; Angus McBride 94–95bc, 98bl, 99cl; Doreen McGuinness (Garden Studios) 48b; Jamie Medline 116bl; Chris Molan (Main) 90tr, 97br, 101br; Steve Noon (Garden Studios) 78b, 126b; Nicki Palin 9cl; Alex Pang 80tr, 90tl, 91tl; Darren Pattenden 42cl, 42bl, 43l; Andie Peck 33tl; Neil Reed 60cl; Eric Robson 18–19b, 20tr, 21tr; Eric Rowe 33cl; Michael Rowe 14c, 16–17t, 16cr, 23tr, 30cl, 38tr; Valerie Sangster 9tr; Mike Saunders (Julian Burgess) 52tr, 96tr; Nick Shewring (Garden Studio) 81b; Brian Smith 117cr; Guy Smith (Mainline Design) 70c, 71l, 71br; M Stacey 73cl; Roger Stewart 40tl, 58tl, 63cl, 63cr, 72br, 92tl, 110tl; Charlotte Styles 71br; Treve Tamblin 18tr, 20cr; Ian Thompson 84bl; Shirley Tourret 100tr; Chris Turnbull 20br; Vincent Wakerley 46bl; Helen Ward (Virgil Pomfret Agency) 38–39b, 39r; Richard Ward 70l; Ross Watton (Garden Studios) 47b; Phil Weare (Linden Artists) 15cl, 15b; Gareth Williams 127cr; Joanna Williams 113cr, 118bc; Ann Winterbotham 68–69b; Dan Wright 21c, 31c; David Wright (Kathy Jakeman) 14b; Paul Wright 49t; Jurgen Ziewe 87cl

Cartoons: Mike Davies 104; Ian Dicks 8, 16, 88, 90; Tony Kenyon (B. L. Kearley) 12, 18, 20, 24, 26, 36, 56, 60, 62, 64, 72, 74, 76, 78, 82, 84, 86, 96, 98, 116, 118, 120, 122, 124, 126; Anthony Lewis 30, 66; Kevin Maddison 68; Peter Wilkes (SGA) 10, 22, 28, 34, 46, 48, 50, 54, 102, 106, 108